T0193567

Also by Doug Zipes

Nonfiction
Into Africa
Taking Ban on Ephedra

Fiction
Stolen Hearts (short story with Joan Zipes)
The Black Widows (a novel)
Ripples in Opperman's Pond (a novel)
Not Just a Game (a novel)

Medical Textbooks (coeditor, coauthor)
Comprehensive Cardiac Care (seven editions)
The Slow Inward Current and Cardiac Arrhythmias
Cardiac Electrophysiology and Arrhythmias
Nonpharmacologic Therapy of Tachyarrhythmias
Treatment of Heart Diseases
Catheter Ablation of Cardiac Arrhythmias
Antiarrhythmic Therapy: A Pathophysiologic Approach
Arrhythmias and Sudden Death in Athletes
Electrophysiology of the Thoracic Veins
Sudden Death: A Handbook for Clinical Practice
Heart Disease: A Textbook of Cardiovascular Medicine (seven editions)
Cardiac Electrophysiology: From Cell to Bedside (seven editions)
Clinical Arrhythmology and Electrophysiology
Electrocardiography of Arrhythmias
Case Studies in Electrophysiology

Medical Articles
More than 850 authored/coauthored

DAMN
THE
NAYSAYERS

A DOCTOR'S MEMOIR

DOUG ZIPES, MD

DAMN THE NAYSAYERS
A DOCTOR'S MEMOIR

The views expressed in this work are solely those of the author and do not necessarily reflect the views of the publisher, and the publisher hereby disclaims any responsibility for them.

iUniverse books may be ordered through booksellers or by contacting:

iUniverse
1663 Liberty Drive
Bloomington, IN 47403
www.iuniverse.com
1-800-Authors (1-800-288-4677)

Because of the dynamic nature of the internet, any web addresses or links contained in this book may have changed since publication and may no longer be valid. The views expressed in this work are solely those of the author and do not necessarily reflect the views of the publisher, and the publisher hereby disclaims any responsibility for them.

Any people depicted in stock imagery provided by Thinkstock are models, and such images are being used for illustrative purposes only.
Certain stock imagery © Thinkstock.

ISBN: 978-1-5320-3311-7 (sc)
ISBN: 978-1-5320-3313-1 (hc)
ISBN: 978-1-5320-3312-4 (e)

Library of Congress Control Number: 2017918623

Print information available on the last page.

iUniverse rev. date: 01/31/2018

FOREWORD
TO
DAMN THE NAYSAYERS
A DOCTOR'S MEMOIR

I have found that most academic physician-scientists are pretty dull people. In order to meet their multiple responsibilities—to their families, patients, students, research fellows, and institutions, to secure funds and to conduct their research—little time or energy is left for other activities. Also, in order to be successful, they have to play along with the system in which they work. Not so for my friend and esteemed colleague Douglas Zipes. Doug is unquestionably the leading clinical electrophysiologist and arrhythmologist (a physician who specializes in the diagnosis and management of patients with disorders of cardiac rhythm) of the present era. His research is published in more than 850 medical papers, many of which are landmarks in the field. He has authored and edited the most important books and journals in cardiology, and his reputation as a clinician, lecturer, and teacher has brought him many prestigious awards, as well as VIP patients and outstanding trainees from all over the world.

An important thread in Doug's professional life is that he is first and foremost a physician whose goal has always been improving the care of the patient—whether it is in the laboratory studying a new drug on isolated heart muscle, in the clinical electrophysiologic laboratory studying and treating patients with a potentially fatal arrhythmia, at the bedside teaching medical students, when delivering a key lecture to thousands of physicians at a World Congress, or when evaluating a scientific paper or a chapter in a book that he edits.

Several characteristics set Doug apart from other successful physician-scientists. He is an adventurer—while visiting the Soviet Union he tangled with the KGB, he has made a "house call" to Saudi Arabian royalty, and he has served as an expert witness for both defense and plaintiff (whichever he thought was right), in high-profile cases that involved drugs and devices and many millions of dollars in potential damages. He has fought, usually successfully, device companies whose equipment was flawed or the instructions on how to use it were inadequate. Doug has powerful ethical values that drive his behavior. In an effort to do the right thing, he is prepared to stand his ground whether it is with a distinguished professor, a multibillion- dollar corporation, or the secret police of the Soviet Union.

Doug has another side that distinguishes him from his peers. He is a remarkable storyteller. His three science fiction novels, as well as this memoir, uncover a previously hidden talent. Of course, he has not been alone on this journey. His companion, Joan—Doug's charming wife of more than a half century—has been his anchor and source of strength along with being a most effective managing editor of his journals.

This memoir will be of great interest to many—including students and more advanced trainees who want to know what goes into establishing a successful career in academic cardiology, the wider public who has wanted to look under the hood of the important yet sometimes obscure world of academic medicine, and, perhaps most important, the thousands of people whose lives have been touched by this remarkable man.

Eugene Braunwald, MD
Distinguished Hersey Professor of Medicine
Harvard Medical School

CONTENTS

PART III MEDICAL EDUCATION AND TRAINING

PART IV PATIENTS AND LITIGATION

PART V INDUSTRY

PART VI ORGANIZATIONS

PART VII HEALTH RISKS

PART VIII WRITING FOR GOOD TIMES AND BAD

PREFACE

No, you can't.

Those three words have shaped a lot of my life's journey—at times angering, occasionally dissuading, but always challenging me to come to terms with who I am, where I want to go, and what I want to be. Life's easier when "Yes, you can" paves the way, but the true test of a person is the challenge to damn the naysayers and do it anyway.

Just as an author's personal memories influence his fiction, all memoirs inevitably contain some fiction that often speaks the truth. The details of my life that I've presented here are as I remember them. However, selective retention undoubtedly colors any recall. Two viewers of the same scene often recount entirely different versions, especially of an event that occurred years earlier. The verbal exchanges I've written capture the essence of the conversations, but my memory is too fallible to recollect each word for word. I have not reviewed my trial transcripts, so those court scenes are also presented entirely from memory. The precise wording may be faulty, but my emotions as I've described them, as well as the outcomes of the trials, have been recounted accurately.

For this to be a true memoir, it must be told from my memory, from my subjective recollection of events, shaded by my point of view, by who I am and the facts as I remember them. Fidelity to my subjectivity should be the objective of the memoir. Otherwise, the reader could just Google the details, or at least some of them, and what fun would that be? However, I am reminded by Marcel Proust that "Remembrance of things past is not necessarily the remembrance of things as they were."

I have organized the memoir so that major changes in time, events, and places are not too jarring. The memoir has no definitive ending, nor should it, as my life goes on, and I continue to damn the naysayers. However, I seem to hear the words "No, you can't" a lot less frequently than I did years ago.

ACKNOWLEDGMENTS

I am indebted to my editor, friends, and family who read drafts, picked up errors, and made great suggestions: Clair Lamb; Michael Rosen; Nancy Stephenson; and my children Debra, Jeffrey, and David. And to my publisher, iUniverse, for outstanding professionalism and expertise. As always, my wife, Joan, did the yeoman's work, at home and for the memoir. This memoir is dedicated to my family and all my friends and nonfriends who have made my life an interesting journey.

PART I

USSR

REFUSENIKS

"Are you Douglas Zipes, the heart specialist from Indiana?" the deep voice over the phone asked, setting in motion the most terrifying yet rewarding series of events in my entire life.

I sat down on the side of the bed—collapsed, really—in my tiny room in the Rossiya Hotel. I had just checked in after a long flight from the States. Who could know I was here already? Was someone watching me? Were all the stories I had heard about being spied on in the USSR true? I knew from my previous travels to the USSR in 1977 that nothing was truly private here.

It was Sunday morning, June 20, 1982, and I had arrived in Moscow for the World Congress of Cardiology hosted by my friend Evgeny Chazov. I had met Chazov in 1977 during my first two trips to Moscow. He was the most important and prominent cardiologist in the entire USSR, head of Moscow's All-Union Scientific Center of Cardiology, recipient of multiple state prizes, and personal physician to heads of state, including Brezhnev, Chernenko, Andropov, and Yeltsin. In addition to being a leading clinician, he was the first in the world to show that a clot-buster could interrupt a patient's heart attack. This observation paved the way to modern treatment with catheters and stents to open clogged arteries in heart attack victims.

I had checked into the famed Rossiya Hotel, built in the 1960s as a five-star international hotel. The Rossiya was gigantic, the largest hotel in the world at that time, with more than 3,500 rooms and suites to accommodate more than four thousand guests. Though plentiful, many rooms were little bigger than walk-in closets with a bathroom. The Rossiya sat adjacent to Red Square, a stone's throw from the Kremlin, and even housed a secret police station with unmarked jail cells. Lodging in those rooms was free, though the stay probably exceeded the few days I planned.

Gray-haired little old ladies (LOLs) sat behind worn wooden desks on each hotel floor every hour of every day. The LOLs had a clear view of who walked into and out of each hotel room. When guests left their rooms, they would hand the LOL their hotel keys. She would return them when they came back. She logged each entry and exit next to the guest's name on a sheet of paper locked in a desk drawer.

As if that kind of snooping weren't enough, I had been warned that all the rooms were bugged. A friend who had visited the hotel the year before said that he'd shivered in bed under a thin blanket one night and complained aloud about how cold the room was. Moments later, the heat in his room flicked on.

"Are you Douglas Zipes?" the caller asked again.

"Who wants to know?" I responded.

"My name is not important," he replied. "Just that I am a refusenik. That's all that matters. You know what that is?"

"Yes," I said. I knew refuseniks were Jews who tried to get an exit visa to leave the USSR and were refused. They lost their jobs and incomes and could not attend meetings, do their research, or publish their papers.

"We are in a jail without bars," he said. "If we don't get some sort of job, the government labels us parasites or hooligans, and then they can do almost anything they want to us, like make us leave Moscow or put us in prison. So we work in any position, cleaning toilets, sweeping streets, whatever."

2

"I'm sorry for that. But why are you calling me?" I began to think maybe this was some sort of a prank, one of my colleagues faking a Russian accent. I was tempted to hang up and move on with the duties that had brought me to Moscow, but I was curious and intrigued by the caller.

"How brave are you? We need someone with courage."

I gulped. Not likely a prank. I didn't like the way this conversation was going, though I must admit I felt a sense of adventure. Still, this was the Soviet Union, and the phone line was likely tapped. The caller seemed to share my concern.

"I am calling from a pay station outside your hotel. I cannot enter the Rossiya—it is strictly forbidden for Russians without special permission papers. If you come down to the sidewalk now, I will find you, and we can talk more. I will approach you holding a folded magazine under my right arm so you will know it is me. Moscow's Jewish scientists are depending on you. Please come."

I knew the LOL on my floor would track my leaving and return, and the caller might be caught outside and questioned by police. But he had to have known that and was still taking the risk. If he really was a refusenik and willing to accept that, so was I.

Pedestrian traffic clogged the sidewalk around the Rossiya as I walked among the tourists. The weather was just turning warm, and the sun was melting a few remaining patches of snow protected in shadows behind bushes and buildings. I was a bit anxious that I might be detained by the KGB, but I felt reasonably safe lost in the crowd of people.

Several *beryozka* stores—upscale stores reserved for non-Russians—teemed with tourists. These stores sold products unavailable to Soviet citizens for hard currency. Tables were piled high with Russian fur hats—*ushanka*—rows of painted nesting dolls, and silver spoons with a Moscow city emblem. Lacquered boxes, pendants, and trays displayed intricate, colorful figures on a glossy black background, illustrating Russian fairy tales. Religious icons and replicas from Saint Basil Cathedral adorned the walls. And of course, there were lots and lots of bottles of Stolichnaya vodka.

Street-food kiosks sold stuffed potatoes and *blinchiki*, a toasted Russian crepe, and filled the air with delicious aromas. The longest lines queued in front of the ice cream booths hawking rich, creamy scoops of vanilla or chocolate. Stalls next to them peddled kvass, a national drink, from large wooden barrels sitting on the sidewalk. The proprietor poured the sweet red liquid into a squat glass secured by a short chain to the kiosk. After the customer drank, the owner rinsed the glass with water from a pitcher, wiped the rim with a rag that once was white, and filled it with kvass for the next customer. The proprietor offered me a glass, but I politely declined. I lost my thirst at that moment.

I stood in front of the kvass booth thinking how that would play with sanitation officials in the United States, when a man wearing a hat low over his eyes bumped into me. I grabbed for my wallet, but that was not necessary. He cradled a magazine under his right arm.

"Excuse me," he said in Russian-accented English. "You are Dr. Zipes, yes?"

I nodded.

"I am Viktor. Please to walk alongside me so we can talk."

I stood, hesitant, studying his face. He was about my height, maybe five foot nine or ten, slim, clean-shaven, with expressive brown eyes that seemed intelligent and kind. His lined face and wisps of gray hair beneath the brown cap put him in his midfifties, although Russians often looked much older than their age. He wore an open-necked blue shirt and dark pants.

As we walked, Viktor cast a wary look around and tossed the magazine into a trash can. He started to take my arm to guide me into a side street but thought better of it as we approached a long line of people standing patiently in front of a store.

"Why are they in line?" I asked.

Viktor shrugged. "I don't know, and most of them don't either. When a Russian sees a group of people queuing, he just gets in line, hoping it will lead to a new delivery of fresh vegetables, maybe some meat, or even toilet paper. Everyone carries string bags to be prepared for such an occasion to happen."

He led the way with a head nod. When the strollers thinned out, he said, "Here it is more quiet, and we can talk without someone to look at us. It is forbidden for us to talk to foreigners."

We walked along in silence for several minutes. Viktor glanced around a half-dozen times until we were totally alone on the street, away from all the hubbub.

He held out his hand and formally introduced himself. "I know you are a cardiologist, but you don't know me. I was a mathematician scientist, chairman of my department at the university. I applied for an exit visa, but the government claimed I knew state secrets and could not be trusted to leave. So they took away my job, and now I sweep city streets. They said I must wait ten years until the secrets are no longer useful. Then I can reapply."

"That's awful," I said.

He shrugged. "It happened to all of us." He swept a hand around.

"All of whom?" I didn't know what I was getting into and had to find out before this went any further. I was in Moscow to lecture at the World Congress of Cardiology, not to be involved in some sort of clandestine activity. Still, I was intrigued and wanted to help if I could.

"I will explain," he said. "Two years ago, we started the Sunday Seminars."

He looked at me to see whether that registered. He continued when he saw my blank look.

"We formed a group of about thirty scientists with various specialties. We were all refuseniks denied access to our jobs and laboratories. Some of us were even members of the Russian Academy of Science and had won the Stalin Prize. RAS only accepted the leading intellectuals. We could read no journals or newspapers. Admission to the public library was denied. We could not attend scientific meetings of any kind."

"Like this World Congress?"

"Exactly. So, when a major scientific meeting was going to be held in Moscow, one of us would invite a visiting scientist to give us a private lecture. We usually did this on Sundays. The subject matter was unimportant. We are all so starved for science; anything new would do. We did this in the apartment of my friend—"

He stopped short. I looked at him, but his eyes were fixed, staring straight ahead.

A man approached from the opposite direction. He was tall and thick-shouldered, wearing a suit, tie, and hat despite the warm day. He'd been walking quickly but slowed as he neared. My new acquaintance stiffened, a look of fear flashed across his face, and he moved several feet away from me. The man advanced, stopped in front of him, and then walked between us. He squinted at Viktor and me—long, penetrating stares. I could almost hear a camera clicking on and off in his head. He continued past us in slow motion, then craned his head around for another look over his shoulder before he turned the corner.

I felt my heart race, though not a word had transpired and the man made no overt moves against us. Perhaps that made it even worse, just the intimidation of his presence. It was an encounter of understated terror.

"What was that about?" I asked, a tremor in my voice.

Viktor shook his head. "I don't know, but there are KGB agents all around, and you have to be alert every minute. Like I said, we are not supposed to talk to foreigners. I could be arrested."

Viktor tried to appear nonchalant, but his hands were trembling and his forehead was moist. After his breathing slowed, he continued, his voice barely a whisper.

"So, we held these Sunday Seminars and learned all kinds of new things happening all over the world. It was wonderful." He paused.

"And?" I prompted.

"The apartment was pretty far out of town, in the—how do you say—outskirts?"

I nodded.

"In the outskirts of Moscow, and we thought we were safe. One evening during the lecture, a fierce pounding rattled the door, and the KGB burst in. They arrested us and took us to jail. They kept us in a jail cell overnight and then let us go. But the owner of the apartment—a well-known physicist named Victor Brailovsky — was arrested November 13, 1980, held for ten months in a Moscow prison, then exiled for three years to Kazakhstan. That ended the Sunday seminars."

"I'm so sorry. That must've been difficult for all of you."

"Yes. We lost a colleague and have had no seminars for two years. We feel so out of touch with the world. We're starved for what is happening. That is why I wanted to talk with you."

I could feel the surge of adrenalin as I saw where this was going. He was sucking me in like quicksand, way over my head. I didn't know this man from Adam, didn't know if I could trust him, didn't know if I was being set up. If I'd ever faced a "no, you can't" or maybe a "no, you shouldn't" situation, this was it. I should have considered this before I agreed to meet him.

I drew a deep breath to calm down and took another look at Viktor. He seemed an honest and sincere guy. Why would he set me up? For what? Didn't make sense. But just how big a risk was I taking?

"So, what do you think?" Viktor asked, breaking into my thoughts.

He must have seen the initial panic on my face. He patted my shoulder. "I know about you from your last visit," he said. "One of our doctors met you in Moscow in 1977 and said you could be trusted."

"Trusted? To do what?" I asked, my voice tremulous. I knew what he was going to ask, but I had to hear it to believe it.

"To be our first scientist to restart our Sunday Seminars."

I heard the words with a mixture of elation at being chosen by these premier scientists and fright at the risk it entailed. Was I being naïve about the risks? I was in Moscow, not comfortable, safe Indianapolis.

"Come," he said, again taking my elbow, then linking his arm in mine. He guided me to yet another side street where a lone café sat buried among a small nest of trees. A green awning spanning its entrance blended with the foliage, making it hard to spot despite the blazing sun in the cloudless sky overhead.

Viktor nodded in its direction. "A friend runs this. We can have a nice tea and talk without strangers to listen."

We entered the tiny shop where the proprietor, a short, stout man with a long gray beard and bald head, stood behind a small counter. Red and brown stains streaked the front of a long white apron. He glanced up from polishing glasses, inspecting each in the window's light. He stacked them on the counter where they caught the sun's rays and twinkled in rainbow colors.

The proprietor untied the apron and bunched it on the counter. He came forward and greeted Viktor in Russian. Viktor replied and nodded at me. The man smiled, shook my hand, and led us to a table tucked in a secluded corner I hadn't even seen. Furthest from the door, the table was hidden in shadows. Half a dozen empty tables filled the rest of the floor space. My mind was ablaze with conflicting thoughts of home, work, and the thrill of an adventure beyond anything I could imagine.

We sat. In two minutes, steaming cups of very dark tea appeared on the table, along with a loaf of black bread and a large bottle without a label that looked like water. I knew better. Neither of us reached for the vodka at eleven in the morning.

Viktor ripped off a chunk of bread, dipped it in his tea, and began chewing. "Eat," he said, nodding at the bread. "It is almost lunchtime." I followed suit.

"Let me explain," Viktor said, swallowing another chunk of bread. "We knew you were a featured speaker here and knew you arrived this morning."

"How?" I asked.

"We have a source in the World Congress administration. I have a friend who has an apartment on the outskirts of Moscow, a real quiet neighborhood where it is likely we would be left alone."

I felt my eyebrows rise. Was I hearing things? Maybe an echo? "Didn't you just tell me this story?"

He nodded with a sheepish smile.

"What's different this time?" I asked.

He made circles with his teacup. "Maybe nothing, maybe everything. It is two years later, and maybe the KGB does not care anymore. I cannot give you a guarantee, but if the KGB comes, they will probably leave you alone. At most, you would get a gentle interrogation."

"What's gentle?"

"Just a little talking."

"What happened to the visiting scientist two years ago when the KGB raided?" I asked.

"He was questioned for a few hours and released." Viktor shifted uncomfortably in his seat and wrinkled his forehead. I began to wonder if he was being forthright and telling me the truth.

"And what could happen to you?"

He blew on his tea and sipped, ripped off another bread chunk, and talked with bulging cheeks. "There is no prediction. They could arrest us or just give us a warning and close down the apartment."

"And the owner?"

"He takes the biggest risk."

"Who would come to this Sunday Seminar?" I asked.

"All refusenik scientists with no jobs, phones disconnected, mail intercepted, and no scientific meetings since the arrest. We are hungry for new science of any kind."

I thought about that for a moment. Why would they want a lecture from me? I was a clinical cardiologist who took care of patients. Although I did experimental research in a basic laboratory, I doubted it was on the hard-core level of these scientists. In college, I had had a difficult time getting a decent grade in physics, and now I was to lecture world-class Russian mathematicians and physicists? That gave me as much a chill as anticipating a KGB raid.

"I'm a cardiologist."

"We know. We also know you have published basic research on the heart. That's what we would like to hear about—your basic work. I think that is what you are scheduled to lecture about to the World Congress."

I took a sip of tea and pushed the cup away. The tea had grown cold.

My thoughts were on my family, my wife and three children in Indiana. Here I was in Moscow, sitting in a tiny café on a side street near Red Square with a man I'd known for less than an hour, asking me to do something my wife—and I guess I as well—would consider crazy. Not just crazy but *absolutely crazy*. I supposed that this escapade had two extremes. It might end up ruining my life or give me the opportunity to contribute in ways I could never have dreamed.

I also had a responsibility to the World Congress organizers who had invited me to lecture and paid all my expenses. I could envision the KGB raiding the apartment during my lecture, arresting me, and the newspapers the next day publishing a picture of me being led off in handcuffs.

Did I have an overactive imagination or a glimpse of reality? I couldn't tell.

The proprietor interrupted my thoughts with a fresh, hot cup of tea. I nodded my thanks as he removed the old cup.

"Do you have enough courage to do this for us, Dr. Zipes?"

It was as if Viktor had read my mind. How terribly unjust for these scientists to be denied their life's work simply because they were Jews and wanted to leave the USSR. True, they were not being tortured or killed, but they were in a political prison for at least ten years, maybe longer, starved for new knowledge. I could bring them a bit of intellectual nourishment, some daylight from the outside world.

Am I so vulnerable to such taunts? I wondered. *Someone says, "No, you can't," and I have to respond, "Yes, I can"?*

I took a moment to answer. "If I do, do you have enough courage to show up?"

He didn't blink. "I and twenty-nine others will be there."

"Where and when?"

"Tomorrow at two o'clock."

"Tomorrow's Monday," I said.

He smiled. "For you we'll rename them the Monday Meetings."

"Thanks."

"The apartment is hard to find, and I would like to introduce you to a friend who will meet you tomorrow and take you to the apartment."

"Who is this?" I asked, my suspicion resurfacing. Why couldn't Viktor take me? Why did he want to bring me to meet another person? To lead me to another part of Moscow? The thought passed through my mind that this was an elaborate plot to kidnap me for ransom. After all, if the refuseniks were unemployed or held trivial jobs, they could use the money. Was I being ridiculous or sensible? Was he really a refusenik?

"You still don't trust me, do you?"

"I'm sorry; it's just—"

He interrupted with a wave of his hand. "I understand. I really do. The man I will take you to now will show you we are all friends you can trust."

"Who is he?"

"Naum Meiman. Naum was awarded the Stalin Prize for his work in theoretical and experimental physics. Almost like the Nobel Prize. He lost all when he and his wife, Inna, applied for exit visas. He became a refusenik and a member of the Helsinki Watch Group."

I shook my head, perplexed.

"A human rights group in Moscow, formed after the Helsinki Accords in 1975. Naum wrote many documents for them—letters of protest that he published in the West, even though the KGB watched him and Inna every minute. He smuggled them out somehow."

My thoughts were in turmoil. What in God's name was I getting into? This was all moving too fast. If the KGB was watching this man, would they watch me as well?

"Come," Viktor said, gripping my arm. "It is a short ride on the underground to his apartment."

Viktor laid some rubles on the table and pushed his chair back. That brought the proprietor running over. He swept up the money and jammed it into Viktor's pocket, saying something loud in Russian with a shake of his head and a waggled finger. Viktor shrugged and smiled his thanks. They shook hands.

I watched this interaction between obvious friends. The open sincerity and trust reassured me. Even so, how dangerous would it be? I stood and shook hands with the proprietor. He held my hand a long time, then covered it with his other hand. The gesture spoke volumes. I began to believe in Viktor and what was happening.

Viktor could not guarantee the outcome or my safety, but whatever happened, I felt good, deep in my gut, that this was the right decision. I had to make my contribution, however small, to help these scientists.

2

NAUM AND INNA MEIMAN

The Moscow metro, opened before WWII and expanded in the years after, is a marvel of engineering. Artists, architects, and engineers collaborated to create stations with marble walls, sparkling crystal chandeliers, splendid artwork, and porcelain bas reliefs depicting the daily life of the Soviet worker. An army of LOLs scrubbed each station, so if your pants were dirty, you felt embarrassed sitting on a pristine white marble bench while waiting for the next train, and compelled to brush it off after you stood.

Viktor guided me through turnstiles, down and up steep, shiny escalators as my head swiveled to take in the beautiful surroundings. No graffiti had been scrawled on these walls, and no cigarette butts or dirty papers littered the floor.

After two stops and a change of trains, we exited on a broad city street, two lanes in either direction separated by a wide median of tall grass, browned by the sun. A minicity of six apartment buildings, each fifteen or twenty floors, formed a semicircle off the main street. No flowers but lots of scraggly grass and shrubs, and well-worn dirt paths crisscrossing lawns in need of weeding, mowing, and watering.

Colorful wash hung from ropes stretched between windows high above, from pink panties and bras to workmen's blue shirts. We heard one window pop open and looked up to see a woman wring out a pair of overalls, reel in her line over a pulley, and nip the blue pants in place with wooden clothespins.

12

"Don't walk too close to the buildings," Viktor warned belatedly as a torrent of water plunged from the window.

I followed him into the lobby of one apartment building. The hallway reeked with a moldy smell of old food and sweat. Few working-class Russians could afford to use deodorant.

Viktor held a finger to his lips. "No talking until we're inside the apartment," he whispered. "Thin walls have big ears."

He pressed the elevator button. "Sometimes it works, sometimes it doesn't," Viktor said under his breath, hitting the button several more times. Today we were lucky.

Viktor opened the elevator door, pulled back a screen, and we entered a tiny space that might fit four skinny people holding their breath. The elevator lurched upward five floors and ground to a stop with a groan that predicted its demise in the very near future. Viktor yanked the screen, pushed open the elevator door, and walked to the nearest apartment. He knocked twice. The apartment door opened immediately, and a stocky man spread his arms to envelop him.

Naum Meiman was several inches shorter than I, with a slight paunch and a big smile. Bushy gray eyebrows almost held more hair than his head, which showed a shiny forehead and a halo of gray. His full red lips parted in a genuine "glad to see you" beam. I guessed he was in his early seventies.

Naum Meiman and author, Tel Aviv, 1988.

13

He and Viktor began speaking Russian in low tones when a woman with an even larger smile interrupted them. She was shorter than Naum, with an ample bosom and thick waist. Specks of gray flecked her full head of auburn hair. She looked younger than Naum.

"I'm Inna Meiman," she said with no trace of an accent. She stood in front of me and put a hand on each of my shoulders. "I don't know you yet, but I'm sure I'm going to like you," she said, pulling me down to kiss each cheek.

I felt my awkwardness melt in the face of such genuine warmth and hospitality. Something about Inna, her infectious smile, her demeanor—something—just radiated a grandmotherly warmth. All she needed was a plate of warm chocolate-chip cookies and a glass of milk and, as a kid, I could have curled up in her lap, closed my eyes, and rested my head against her chest.

"Hi," I said.

Naum shook my hand while Inna put an arm around my waist, steering me into their living room. I was surprised at its size and well-appointed furniture.

"Where did you learn such impeccable English?" I asked.

"I'm an English teacher," Inna said, with a shake of her head. "Or was. I've written a textbook on advanced English for Russians. I've never been out of Russia, but I've listened to a lot of American tapes."

I was impressed. I'm good at picking up accents and deducing people's origins, but she would have had me fooled.

"Please sit down," Inna said, motioning me to a tan-colored leather sofa along one wall. A polished brass coffee table stood in front of the sofa.

Naum sat beside me. Viktor pulled up a chair in front of us while Inna went off to the kitchen, returning with a tray of tea and cookies—not chocolate chip—that she placed on the coffee table. She poured three cups of tea and motioned for us to take one. "And do try the cookies. I baked them this morning," she said. Naum handed me a cup and turned up the volume on the radio. I could barely hear him over the noise. But no one else could either.

"Viktor told you about the Sunday Seminars?" Naum asked in a soft voice.

"He did," I said, nodding at Viktor.

"And you have agreed to help us?"

"I have, but I must tell you, Naum, I have concerns for my safety and yours," I said.

"As you should," Naum replied. "But we cannot just sit and let the government prevent us from learning new science. Besides, if the KGB does come, they will be more interested in me than you. They watch me pretty closely these days, and I'm sure they have planted a bug in my apartment, so they may know already what we are planning." He raised his eyebrows and looked around the living room as if searching for a recording device.

"Really?" I asked, my heart doing a flip-flop.

"I have searched for them and found one I think they meant for me to find. I'm sure there are others. The KGB is very smart when it comes to things like that." He turned the radio volume up a notch. "A friend of mine had his shoes repaired, and they came back with a transmitter embedded in the right heel. It was so small it looked like a tiny nail in the heel. He never saw it until he stepped in a puddle and it started to screech."

Naum paused a moment, scratched an earlobe, and asked, "What is your lecture for the World Congress?"

"Our latest studies on the calcium current."

"That will be perfect," Naum said.

"I have two-by-two slides," I said, concerned they might not be able to project them.

"No problem. We will bring a projector and a screen. They were the last things I took before I got fired."

He saw the worried look on my face.

"I will meet you in front of your hotel tomorrow at twelve thirty. You're at the Rossiya?"

I nodded.

"It will take us about fifteen minutes to walk to the metro, forty-five minutes on the train to get to the apartment, and then a few minutes to set everything up. You should be ready to lecture at two. How's that?"

My heart beat hard in my chest. It seemed that this was going to happen. Too late for me to get cold feet. "How long should I lecture?"

"You have the whole afternoon, so maybe an hour, then a fifteen-minute break, and then another hour for questions? Or is that too much for you? I'm sure there will be lots of questions."

"That'll be okay." I checked my watch. I had a date for dinner with colleagues at the hotel.

Viktor rose. "I think it is time to take him back to the Rossiya."

Inna came over, sat down beside me, and patted my hand. "It will be fine," she said. "You will be fine. The authorities won't want a big blowup during the World Congress. You're too important for something like that to happen."

I raised one eyebrow, a bit skeptical about my own importance. "Will you be there?" I asked. Her mothering presence was a comfort in the midst of all this scary intrigue.

She shook her head. "I'm an English teacher and wouldn't have any idea what you were talking about. No, I will leave Sunday Seminars to the scientists—even on a Monday. But I will meet you after your lecture and will have a surprise waiting."

"Inna, not now," Naum said, a warning tone in his voice.

"Just a little bit of encouragement," Inna said, smiling.

I had no idea what she was talking about. Frankly, if I came out of this unscathed, that would be surprise enough for me.

3

SUNDAY SEMINAR LECTURE

I returned to the hotel, went to my room, and unlocked my briefcase. It was one of those leather, rectangular boxlike affairs with three file separators inside the top of the briefcase and plenty of room in the bottom. I checked my slides, holding each to the light of the lamp to make sure the order was correct and to review what I planned to say. I had backup slides in a separate pile bound by a rubber band.

I canceled my dinner plans. I was too excited to have an appetite and didn't want to field inevitable questions about why I wasn't eating. I went to bed early. Sleep wouldn't come, despite a sleeping pill. The seven-hour time difference and my excitement were messing with my normal sleep cycle.

I lay staring at the ceiling, asking myself if what I was doing was sane—not just for me but for my family at home. Deep down I knew it was the right thing to do, but was I doing it for my ego, playing to the elusive Walter Mitty in me, perhaps jeopardizing my reputation and even my safety? If the KGB did come and arrest me—no matter how trivial the charges—I would have hell to pay at home, with my university, with the NHLBI and the exchange program, perhaps even with my cardiology practice.

But how could I turn my back on such courageous people who first risked all to leave the USSR and then risked prison for a bit of scientific knowledge from the outside world? The question hung unanswered as I fell asleep around two in the morning.

I spent the morning attending other lectures at the World Congress. It was hard to concentrate on the presentations. I couldn't stop thinking about the refuseniks not being allowed into these halls and my meeting with them later that day.

I thought about what might happen if we had visitors during my lecture. That started my heart racing. Did I attempt to flee? I figured that would be impossible. The KGB would certainly have the exits covered. Resist arrest? Also, not likely. I and the others would probably be herded into some waiting van and taken "downtown."

On my first visit in 1977, I had passed the Lubyanka building. It housed KGB headquarters on Dzerzhinsky Street in downtown Moscow. Lubyanka was a large Baroque, rectangular building with a yellow brick facade that had started as an insurance center. After the Bolshevik revolution in 1917, Dzerzhinsky founded the KGB's predecessor, the Cheka secret police, and commandeered the building. Although only four stories, it was dubbed Moscow's tallest building because they said you could see Siberia from its basement. That was where Lubyanka's notorious prison was hidden. My mind spun all sorts of horrific torture scenarios to which I would be subjected. None of this was likely, but thinking about the possibilities held a certain morbid fascination. At this point, I think I was more excited than fearful. I didn't know if that would change in the future, however.

I met Naum at twelve thirty outside the Rossiya. He seemed less nervous than Viktor about walking and talking with a foreigner in public—perhaps his prior run-ins with the KGB afforded him a certain defiant demeanor—and we had a pleasant conversation as we walked through Red Square. Naum gave me a brief geography lesson, pointing out GUM, Moscow's largest state department store on the eastern side of the square. Directly opposite to the west was Lenin's mausoleum, with the

Kremlin behind. The nine domes of spectacular Saint Basil Cathedral to the south always reminded me of colorful, swirling frozen custards. I got chills thinking my grandfather or great-grandfather might have walked this same square a hundred years ago.

As Naum said, the metro took about forty-five minutes. One of the stops near Red Square had a bronze statue of a border guard kneeling on his left knee, his right hand gripping a rifle and his left hugging a dog sitting next to him. Millions of fingers had rubbed the dog's long snout for luck, buffing the dark bronze muzzle into a shiny yellow veneer. I figured it couldn't hurt and added my pat as we walked past. I needed all the good luck I could muster.

We exited on the fringe of a small town. Although no one was around, Naum fell silent, and I followed suit. We walked from the metro entrance down a steep hill toward a building that looked identical to the one in which Naum lived. The same clothes seemed to be hanging on the same lines between the same windows. This time I knew not to walk too close to the building.

Food and body odors hit us as we entered the apartment building. Naum didn't even bother pushing the elevator button, and we walked up three flights. He paused at each landing to catch his breath.

"Angina," he said between huffs, rubbing his chest where it hurt. He pulled out a handkerchief and wiped his forehead. "I ran out of nitroglycerin. It is hard to get."

On the third floor, he stopped again and held on to the banister. "It's the last door down this hallway," he said, nodding to the right. "But wait just a minute."

When his breathing slowed, he led the way to the apartment and knocked three sharp raps. The peephole in the door flashed open and then closed.

The door swung wide, and we walked into a crowd of people crammed into a tiny living room barely large enough to hold a couch and coffee table, a few folding chairs, and an end table. Conversation halted as all eyes swung toward us. Then they applauded, I think for themselves as much as for me. Emotional tension showed on each face. I couldn't know what they were thinking, but they had to be remembering the calamity two years earlier. We were replaying it, hoping—praying—for a different outcome.

As I scanned the room, the full significance of what I was doing hit me. *This is the elite of the Jewish Russian scientific intelligentsia in Moscow. How incredibly brave they are, and how driven to take this chance for the sake of science. And I am playing a part of that history.*

My heart beat like a trip hammer banging my ribs. I tried to slow my breathing, but I was so keyed up I was almost panting. Once I got into my lecture, I hoped I'd regain control, but right now, emotion overwhelmed me. It was a mixture of fear, excitement, and an intellectual high, about to lecture to these brilliant men—perhaps with the KGB waiting outside the door. No women were present. While more than half the Soviet physician workforce was female, the upper echelons of science were mostly men.

Naum walked to the center of the room, his hand gripping my arm to pull me along. He introduced me to the group and said, "Let's hold off individual introductions until the end of the lecture since we don't know how much time we will have." He looked meaningfully at me, then at the apartment door. "If all goes well, there'll be plenty of opportunity later to meet Dr. Zipes and to chat.

"Remember—if we get interrupted, be courteous but courageous. We are doing nothing wrong, just meeting to talk about science. And finally, no political discussions. There could be ears all over." He raised his eyebrows and looked at the ceiling.

A small white screen was already set up at one end of the room alongside a blackboard. At the other end, a slide projector sat on a small table, plugged in and ready to go. People grabbed whatever seating was available. Five crammed onto the sofa, pressing shoulder to shoulder, hip to hip. Others sat on chairs scattered about or sat on the floor. Many just stood along the perimeter of the room, leaning back against the wall or with a foot propped behind them.

Author, with refusenik, Sunday Seminar, 1982.

Author at blackboard, Sunday Seminar, refusenik lecture.

I loaded my slides into the projector, walked to the front of the room, said hello to the group, and began my lecture about cardiac electrophysiology. I started by explaining some fundamental physiology terms that I would ordinarily present to clinicians. Then I laughed, realizing who was in the audience. These scientists could explain those terms to me.

After about ten minutes, a loud knock on the door interrupted my lecture. I froze in midsentence, and all heads swiveled toward the door. Some faces blanched. I think we all held our breaths.

Naum stood, patted the air with his hands to reassure everybody, and put a finger to his lips. He went to the door and looked through the peephole. Then he laughed with a sigh of relief.

"It's Igor," he said, opening the door. "Why are you never on time?" he asked the new arrival, slapping him on the back.

The man shrugged, embarrassed, and walked in. He was elderly, gray haired, and stoop shouldered. Two people made a space for him on the couch, and he plunked down, squeezing between them.

I resumed my lecture. Once I got immersed in the topic, the enormity of what I was doing diminished. I went on for almost an hour, came to the end of my first set of slides, and stopped. "Naum, I think this would be a good time for a break."

"Good idea," Naum said. Everyone stood. Some stretched, and others made their way to the bathroom in the hall.

A middle-aged woman emerged from the kitchen—I assumed it was the apartment owner's wife—with a tray of glasses and cups, and a cold pitcher of kvass. Beads of moisture had collected on its surface, coalescing into rivulets running down the side. It made me realize how hot the apartment was. Air-conditioning was nonexistent, and more than thirty of us were jammed into a tiny space. Heavy blue drapes covered the one window.

No one seemed to notice the heat or stale air. We were all immersed in the science and the suspense of the unknown outcome.

The woman placed everything on the coffee table and returned a moment later with a pot of hot tea and a tray of cookies. People helped themselves to the refreshments, but voices were subdued. We knew we weren't out of the woods yet.

After about ten minutes, Naum asked me, "Ready to go again?" I nodded. "How much longer?" he asked.

"Maybe fifteen or twenty minutes," I said. "I want to leave time for questions."

Naum clapped his hands to get everyone's attention. "Let's reconvene," he said. "Dr. Zipes has about twenty minutes left of his formal presentation. Then we can open it up for questions. Grab a cookie, take your drink, and we can restart."

I stood in front of the room as people made their way back to their seats. Most took the same seat they had had during the previous hour. It always struck me that people did this—returned after a break to where they had been sitting, even in large lecture halls. It was almost as if they had claimed that little bit of turf as their own and were most comfortable going back to the same spot.

I looked from Naum to the apartment door before I started. He just smiled and nodded for me to begin again.

I hurried through the last slides, not wanting to tempt fate any longer than necessary. We hadn't been bothered yet, and I wanted to keep it that way.

When I finished, the questions came. They were insightful and demonstrated the grasp these scientists had of subject matter only peripherally related to their own fields. There was sufficient overlap between what I had presented and their own fields of interest that they had gotten something from my lecture.

After the last question, they applauded again. Naum shushed them, nodding at the door, and the handclapping changed to pantomime. When the gestures died out, people returned to the refreshments, stretched, or took another bathroom break. One by one they drifted toward me, introduced themselves, and began to talk—interestingly, no longer about the science I had presented but about relatives they had in the States. Most had no idea about the size of the United States and asked if I ever bumped into their cousin or uncle who lived in Saint Louis or Chicago. Wasn't that right next to Indianapolis?

They asked me to deliver messages to family members scattered across the United States. *Tell my brother Hershel we had another child, a daughter named Sarah, after our mother. Please tell my son Isaac to send pictures of the wedding. Tell Ely that our father died last year.*

They gave me scraps of paper with names and phone numbers to call when I returned home. My pocket bulged with messages to deliver. I promised each I would call and let their families know how well everyone was doing.

I was exhausted. The adrenaline high had ebbed, and I felt wiped. We had made it through the restart of the Sunday—or Monday—Seminars without interruption, and perhaps that augured well for their future. Relief coursed through me, and I'm sure through everyone else in the room. Perhaps that was why they were talking about relatives.

After a bit, Naum came to my rescue, telling all we had another meeting to attend. This was news to me, but I welcomed the opportunity to stop talking and decompress.

Naum advised everyone to leave in staggered groups of no more than two or three. We were the last to go. I thanked our host and praised him for his courage. He returned the compliment, and we left.

Walking down the stairs was a lot easier than ascending, but we now faced hiking up the steep hill to the metro entrance. "I hate this part of town," Naum said. "There never are any taxis, and I get bad angina climbing the damn hill."

As if on cue, a taxi pulled up, and the driver shouted something in Russian. Naum looked suspicious, put a restraining hand on my arm as we walked toward the cab, and whispered in my ear, "KGB. Keep quiet."

We were silent in the back of the cab. I felt safe with Naum even though the driver was KGB. I was exhausted. I didn't realize how much those two hours had taken out of me. The emotional price was huge, but it was worth it. I felt good inside. I rested my head on the back of the seat and closed my eyes.

After about thirty minutes, Naum nudged me from my reverie, and we exited the cab. Naum paid the driver, and we stood on the sidewalk until the cab was lost in the distance.

"What was that all about?" I asked.

"KGB tracking me," Naum said. "They must have known about the seminar but for some reason did nothing. We were lucky. They wanted to find out where I was going next. We'll walk a bit before we meet our friend. Not that it will do much good. They're bound to find out."

"Where are we going?"

"Do you know the name Ida Nudel?"

I shook my head.

"You're about to meet one of the bravest women I know."

4

THE LETTER

"I'm Ida Nudel," she said as we walked into the apartment. She was a short, slender woman with chestnut hair, gray streaks, and intelligent but compassionate eyes set off by round eyeglass frames.

"Thank you for what you just did for our friends," Ida said. "That was very daring of you."

"Thank you. It's a pleasure to meet you," I said.

Ida had been released several months earlier after serving four years of exile in Siberia for hanging a banner from her Moscow apartment window in 1978 saying, "KGB, give me my visa to Israel." The government charges against her were "malicious hooliganism." She had been a known activist since she was refused an exit visa in 1972, campaigning constantly for the other "prisoners of Zion." They called her Mama and the Angel of Mercy.

Inna walked over and enveloped me in her arms. "I told you I had a surprise after your lecture," she said. Inna put her arm across Ida's shoulder. "This lady is the personification of courage. She fights constantly for the refuseniks."

Inna took me by the hand. "Come inside and have some tea. I have sandwiches also. I expect you're hungry after your lecture."

Though I had missed lunch, that was the first time I had thought about food. A table in the living room held an assortment of sandwiches, a pitcher of kvass, and a pot of tea.

While we ate, Ida talked about her four years in Siberia. She'd lived alone in a frigid log hut and worked as a night guard at a truck yard. All village residents were warned not to associate with her.

"It was hard," she said. "Very cold and very lonely." She shuddered at the memory, and her eyes moistened.

"And now I live a nomad's life, wandering from friend to friend. The KGB will not let me return to my own flat or associate with other refuseniks or foreigners. If they knew I was here talking to you, I could be arrested again and sent back to Siberia. All I want is to join my sister, Elena, in Israel. She got an exit visa in 1972 with her husband and son, but the authorities wouldn't let me go. They said I knew state secrets while working for the Moscow Institute of Planning and Production."

"I'm so sorry," I said. "Is there anything I can do to help?"

Naum took a letter from his coat pocket. He unfolded it and smoothed it out on the table. "You can help me get this letter published in an American journal," he said. "It describes what we are living through—not just the scientists but all the refuseniks."

"No problem," I said, retrieving the camera from my briefcase. "I'll take a picture of it to bring back to the States."

Naum's face paled. Frantically he looked around, spied a radio on a table, flipped it on, and cranked up the volume.

He leaned close to my ear. Over the noise of the music he said, "The KGB has certain limits. Obviously, they know we are all here, including our friend Ida." He glanced at Ida, who smiled. "But I think they will leave her alone because of the international interest in what happened to her and that she just came back from Siberia. But they draw the line on some things. I shouldn't have said anything about the letter without the radio on." He pointed to the ceiling. "My mistake."

Directly overhead I saw a tiny metallic protuberance in the ceiling. "A microphone," he mouthed. Then he said in a loud voice, "No, we don't want you to take any pictures or to be involved in any way. I will handle this."

I nodded and started to put my camera away.

He reached over and stopped my hand. "Take the picture," he mouthed. "And get the letter published."

It was almost seven when I arrived back in Red Square. Naum had put me on the metro with instructions when and where to get off. I wanted to wander around a bit on my own and soak up the sights. I resisted his offer for dinner, despite Inna's reputation as a great cook.

It had been an incredibly exhausting afternoon, and it felt good to stroll aimlessly past Saint Basil Cathedral, stare at its flamboyant splendor, and then walk in front of Lenin's mausoleum. The inevitable line of forty or fifty people waited their turn to get in. From my visit in 1977, I knew that each viewer had just a few minutes to circle Lenin's embalmed body. The whispers were always the same: "I don't believe he's real. I bet it's a wax substitute from Madame Tussauds." I kept looking behind me to see if I were being followed but saw no one and eventually gave it up, thinking I was being too melodramatic.

I continued north past the State Historical Museum, turned the corner to the right, and entered GUM. Rubles were worthless in this department store; only hard currency was accepted for the tourist trade luxury items.

I'm not much of a shopper, so after a brief look, I stopped for a beer, realized I was hungry, and headed back to the Rossiya for dinner. I didn't want to be up too late since I had to lecture at the World Congress in the morning.

I finished dinner close to ten and went to my room in the hotel. When I asked for my key, the LOL on my floor gave me a strange look and then handed it to me. I didn't think much of it until I opened the door to my room. I set my briefcase on the floor and gasped.

The room had been trashed!

Drawers were pulled out and my clothes scattered about, pockets turned inside out. The mattress, stripped of linens, lay askew on the bed frame.

I was stunned. I sat down hard on the bed, my head in my hands. Who had done this? Why?

I opened my briefcase and took out the camera. That was why. Someone obviously thought I had come back to the room after leaving Naum and was looking for the film.

Oh my God! What had I gotten myself into? It had all seemed like an exciting adventure—a bit scary to be sure but still just an adventure. I didn't think I'd come to any harm, though that was always a possibility—remote but still a possibility. But I was a US citizen, and this was the Soviet Union. They didn't imprison US citizens, did they?

Of course, they did.

I tried to calm down, but I was a wreck. My hands shook, and I was sweating. I had to get myself together for my lecture in the morning. Fortunately, I would be using the same slides I showed the refuseniks, so that much was done. But I needed some sleep. I took off my jacket and felt a bulge. The messages from all the refuseniks with phone numbers and names of relatives! What was I going to do with them?

I made sure the door was locked and propped a chair against the doorknob. I undressed and got into bed. I took the film from my camera and put it into the breast pocket of my pajama top. Finally, after much tossing and turning and two sleeping pills, I fell asleep.

The ring of the phone woke me. It seemed as if I had just fallen asleep. I looked at the clock on the night table. Four thirty in the morning. Who the hell could be calling at this hour?

I picked up the receiver and heard … nothing!

Nothing except heavy breathing on the other end—in and out, in and out, like someone straining to catch his breath, a sucked in *innhhhhah* and a drawn out *agghhhah*. Over and over.

"Hello? Hello." No answer, just the deep, labored breaths.

I hung up. Now I was in a total state of panic. Obviously, someone was trying to frighten me—and they had succeeded big time. I was terrified, panicky.

THE KGB

5

I paced up and down in my tiny room and tried to think straight. What should I do? Call home? What good would that do? "Hello, Joan. The KGB just ransacked my room and woke me up early to frighten me. Can you help?" Not likely. She'd end up panicking even more than I.

Call Chazov? No, I'd have to tell him where I'd been, what I'd done.

Call the police? *Ha*, I thought. They *were* the police. The secret police.

Holy shit. This was the KGB—the shield and sword of the Kremlin. They were the instrument of supreme power, protecting those in control and attacking those who threatened. What had I been thinking? They had spies everywhere. They *imprisoned* people. They *tortured* people. They *killed* them or had them killed. And here I was meeting with refuseniks—and not just any refusenik. One who had just been released from Siberian exile and was warned not to meet with foreigners. Another who was under constant surveillance.

Oh, and don't forget trying to smuggle a letter out to the West.

I must have been out of my mind to have done all this. What could I have been thinking?

And I had all those pieces of paper from the refuseniks. How could I let them down and not call their families? But how could I protect them? I couldn't reveal their identities. What if I was caught with all their notes? What would happen to them? And to me?

What in God's name should I do? I had no coherent thoughts, just mental chaos. I was in so deep there seemed no way to pull out now.

I glanced at the clock. It was almost five. Forget sleep. No way. I was wound so tight I could explode any minute. My heart was racing. I was in a cold sweat and breathing so fast I was seeing spots in my peripheral vision. My lecture was at nine in the morning. I was the third speaker, but I had to be in the hall by seven thirty to give the projectionist my slides. Would I be able to concentrate and lecture? Suppose the KGB came in the middle to get me?

A shower. That's what I needed to relax, a hot shower. I stayed in the spray for as long as the hot water lasted. When it cooled, I rinsed off and toweled dry. That helped, and I began to think a little more rationally.

I would keep the film with me. If I was stopped, I would say they were tourist pictures, and if someone demanded I give up the film, I would accidently expose the roll.

How would I do that? I had to stop and think. I could unwind it a bit and when I handed it to someone, I could hold the unwound end and drop the rest. It would unfurl. Maybe. Would it work? I didn't know, but I would try.

The refuseniks notes! What could I do with them?

I'd been writing a scientific manuscript in longhand on a yellow legal pad for my secretary to type when I returned to my office. I was planning to finish it on the plane ride home. Suppose I incorporated their notes as part of the manuscript and then ripped their papers to bits. The KGB undoubtedly had experts that could reassemble the pieces. But suppose I dropped a bit here and another bit there in different trash containers as I walked to my lecture? That should work—unless the KGB was watching me. But I had to take that chance.

Would they accuse me of visiting the refuseniks, especially Ida Nudel? I would deny it. How could I? Maybe they had pictures of me with Naum. Of me with the other refuseniks. With Ida Nudel? Maybe they had a spy planted among the refuseniks. But after all, I'd only given a lecture. Yes, it was to refuseniks, but what could they do to me? I brought no contraband, no Bibles or any religious material, no government propaganda. No, that part would be okay, I thought.

Calmer, I set about incorporating the names, messages, and phone numbers into my manuscript. My handwriting was terrible to begin with, and I made a conscious effort to make it even more illegible. When I finished, I pushed the sheets of manuscript into one of the folders in my briefcase. I doubted anyone would discover them. I tore the refusenik notes into tiny fragments and put them in my pocket for later disposal.

I glanced at the clock. Six thirty. I had better get dressed and leave for the lecture hall. It was a twenty-minute walk.

I finished dressing, grabbed my slides and the film, and left. I crossed Red Square, but this time I paid no attention to the landmarks. I was looking for garbage receptacles. At each one, I deposited a little handful of paper shreds. Anyone watching me—were they?—would have thought I was crazy, zigzagging through Red Square, from trash can to trash can. But I did it until my pocket was empty.

I was so distraught I actually became delusional. *Was that 007 in that alcove up ahead? Was James Bond here to help me? Get me out? My God, I'm losing it.* I thought that guy standing at the corner with the hat on was James. Or was it a KGB agent? I walked faster.

I finally reached the lecture hall, gave my slides to the projectionist, and collapsed in a seat. I couldn't concentrate, thinking about the film in my pocket and how incriminating it would be if I were caught with it. *Shit!* A photo of a refusenik letter asking the West for help. I'd be arrested for sure.

Just then a colleague sat down next to me.

"Hi, Frank," I said. "How're you doing?"

Frank Marcus from Tucson was a fellow cardiologist I'd known for ages. A long time ago, he had tried to recruit me to his department at the University of Arizona. Very nice person, superb cardiologist, and a friend I knew I could trust.

"Nothing much. Behaving myself, seeing the sights. You?" Frank said.

The film was burning a hole in my pocket. I literally could feel heat radiating from it—or so I thought. I didn't think there'd be bugs in this big lecture hall, so I whispered everything to Frank, including the film.

"Look," he said. "I've been a model tourist. I'm leaving for home later today. When the lights dim for the next speaker, pass me the film. No one will suspect me of anything, so I won't have any problem getting through customs with the film. Once I get home, I'll mail it to you, and you can get the letter published. How's that?"

I wanted to hug Frank to death. The weight of an elephant lifted off my chest.

"Thank you so much, Frank. You've saved my life."

"I don't know if it's that dramatic, but I'm glad to help," Frank said.

The lights went down for the first speaker, and I slipped him the film. He put it in his inside coat pocket.

"One other thing, Frank, if it's not too much trouble."

"Sure, no problem. What is it?" Frank asked.

"July first is my wife's birthday. I'm scheduled to go to Saint Petersburg tomorrow sightseeing for a few days, but I told Joan I would be back in the West by July first and would call her on her birthday. Would you call her sometime *after* her birthday—say, on July second or third—and make sure I called July first? If I didn't make the call, I'm in deep shit, probably arrested by the KGB and will need some big-time help."

"Happy to," Frank said.

I could have kissed him I was so relieved.

When it was my turn to present, I gave one of the most animated talks I'd ever given. I felt unburdened, shackle-free, like a guy sentenced to death who'd been reprieved. Maybe not that dramatic but close.

The morning session ended. I thanked Frank again, and I sprinted for open space. I wanted to jump up, kick my heels, and shout; I felt so relieved. I had gotten rid of the notes and the film. The sun was shining, the air was fresh, the grass was green. I was a blithe spirit. Free!

Or was I?

6

ESCAPE TO SAINT PETERSBURG

I left for the airport early the next morning to catch an Aeroflot flight to Saint Petersburg. I was anxious to explore that beautiful city, especially to visit the Hermitage Museum. No phone calls during the night and no suspicious encounters, so I felt unburdened and unconcerned.

Maybe a big mistake.

When I checked in at the airport, the airline agent at the counter said, "Oh, yes, Dr. Zipes, we were expecting you."

My heart sank. Perhaps I hadn't escaped the KGB after all. What had they found out and what were they going to do?

Maybe Frank got stopped with the film. Unlikely, I thought. They had no reason to suspect him of anything, and I would've heard if he'd been stopped. He was probably back in the States with the film in his briefcase.

It was also unlikely that the KGB had found my shredded notes. They would have had to retrieve them from five or six receptacles and then piece them together.

They must have proof of my lecturing to the refuseniks, I thought, *and meeting with Ida Nudel. That must be it. Probably photos.* I hoped she was okay. Returning to Siberia would be horrible.

The young lady asked me to follow her to a VIP lounge. Would the KGB be waiting for me there?

We entered the room. Empty. They probably didn't want to make a scene in front of her.

"Please have a seat," she said. "We'll come and get you. Help yourself to the refreshments." She waved her hand toward the bar on which sat bottles of wine and liquor, sandwiches, and a soup tureen.

She was so pleasant I relaxed a little. But maybe that was what the KGB wanted me to do. Have a few drinks and be ready to talk.

I sat stiffly on the edge of my seat and watched the door, waiting for some big guys to come rushing in. When nothing happened, I got up and started pacing. I searched the ceiling for microphones but didn't see any, not that I really knew what to look for. Without the incriminating film or original refuseniks' notes, I wasn't as anxious as I'd been the morning before, but I was still stressed.

The ticking clock didn't help. I was getting nervous I'd miss my flight, especially if they planned to question me. Maybe that's what they intended—for me to miss the flight.

Finally, with only ten minutes left before takeoff, the young lady entered again, this time with a porter. He tied a large VIP tag to my suitcase and hefted the bag onto a trolley.

The young lady said, "Please follow him to the car. Have a good trip." She smiled and left.

I had no idea what was going on, so I followed the porter. He led me outside to a waiting van and put my bag inside. "Enjoy your good trip, sir," he said and pushed the trolley back into the airport, leaving me standing there.

I had no idea what was going on, but I also had no choice, so I got into the van. As soon as I did, we sped off onto the tarmac toward an Aeroflot plane. The driver stopped at the staircase leading up into the front of the plane. He got out, started up the stairs with my bag, and nodded for me to follow.

The flight attendant met me as I entered the plane. "Good morning, Dr. Zipes," she said. "It's a pleasure to have you join us on our flight to Saint Petersburg. Your seat is waiting." She nodded to the first seat in first class. The plane was totally full except for this seat. "Please sit down. We'll stow your bag up front, and then we're ready to take off."

I was speechless, astonished. Instead of being arrested by the KGB, I was being treated like royalty. I collapsed into the seat. The flight attendant reached over and buckled my seat belt. In moments, I heard the roar of the engines as we accelerated down the runway.

I closed my eyes and tried to piece together an explanation. It had to have been Chazov. He must have saved me. Maybe he had bargained with the KGB, agreeing they could scare me but nothing more. Maybe the KGB had acted independently. Maybe ... maybe. Lots of maybes.

I could guess all I wanted, but I would never know.

Whatever it was, I gave silent thanks to my friend and protector, Evgeny Chazov. He turned out to be my very own James Bond, and I would be indebted to him forever.

7

SAINT PETERSBURG

Czar Peter the Great founded Saint Petersburg, USSR's second largest city, in the early 1700s. Situated on the Neva River with a Baltic Sea port, the beautiful city is the most Westernized in Russia, and is its cultural capital. More than two hundred museums are scattered throughout Saint Petersburg, with the Hermitage Museum, established by Czarina Catherine the Great in 1764, the grandest and oldest.

City officials had arranged a bus tour the afternoon we arrived. We were some forty post-Moscow convention sightseers, mainly from Europe and the United States. Our "guide" was reputed to be a KGB agent, so I was particularly attentive to her directions.

"You will have three hours to tour the museum," she announced over a microphone from the front of the bus as we pulled to a stop near the Winter Palace. "The bus will remain parked in this lot until you return. Please be prompt." She checked her watch. "It is precisely two o'clock, so everyone must be back by five. Understood?"

The group mumbled assent. Most were senior physicians not used to such orders, but we joked about it good-naturedly and went our various ways.

The Hermitage was mind-blowing, with more than three million objects (not all on display) housed in six historic buildings. The Winter Palace was one of the six, a spectacular baroque, green-and-white edifice with 1,500 rooms, built in 1708 on a monumental scale to reflect the imperial power of Russia. One side faced the blue waters of the flowing Neva, and the other a vast courtyard. Bloody Sunday took place in that courtyard in 1905 when the Imperial Guard fired on unarmed demonstrators petitioning Czar Nicholas II for better working conditions. The slaughter triggered a public outcry that helped fuel the 1917 revolution that overthrew the czar, murdering him, his wife, Alexandra, and his children.

I could have spent days or even weeks at the Hermitage—never mind three hours—and still have seen only a fraction of the collection. Of the million works of art, my heart took me to the Impressionists, where I drooled over Renoir, Monet, Van Gogh, Gauguin, Cezanne, Degas, and Sisley. The three hours evaporated in a flash, and I returned to the bus by five along with my colleagues—all except one.

Thirty-nine of us waited and waited on the bus until he returned twenty minutes late.

"I'm so sorry," he said, panting and sweating from his run to the bus. "I got lost and went to the wrong parking lot."

Our guide—revealing her identity or at least her training—responded with classic propaganda. "I hope you all see how the freedom of one imprisons many."

All conversations in the bus halted as her statement struck home. After a few stunned moments, a guy on my left booed, and someone across the aisle hissed. Then we all did. Our guide scrunched up her face, turned her back on the group, and plunked down in her seat in the front of the bus. She switched off her microphone, and we had to identify landmarks from a map as we drove back to the hotel.

At dinner that night, I sat with a group preparing to visit refuseniks. I guess I was a glutton for punishment—or maybe excitement. They had brought presents of food, clothing, toys, and—risky, very risky—religious objects such as mezuzahs, Stars of David, and a few copies of the Old Testament smuggled in from Europe.

"Do you know the risks you're taking?" I asked.

"What risks?" was the reply. "Just harmless visits, giving away trinkets."

"The religious stuff, those are not trinkets. Let me tell you what happened to me in Moscow," I said.

When I finished, I suggested they leave the religious items at the hotel. They thought that was a good idea, but I'm not sure they complied since they gift-wrapped the presents and easily disguised the contents.

We met in the lobby after dinner and walked to the metro in one large group. We were dressed in Western garb and carrying many packages. I felt very conspicuous, but no one else seemed concerned. I was amazed that no one stopped us to ask where we were going or what we were doing.

Perhaps Saint Petersburg was more liberal toward foreigners than Moscow.

Or maybe it was the White Nights.

For eighty days, from May to July, the nonsetting sun kept the city bright long past midnight, and a jovial spirit captured the metropolis and entranced its occupants. Couples got married, and city residents, weary of the long winter, joyously filled restaurants and bars, dancing, singing, and—yes, drinking vodka to the wee morning hours. Opera, classical music, and ballet performances dominated the day, but at night, revelers spilled into the streets for impromptu celebrations à la Bourbon Street in New Orleans.

We split into twos and threes, divided up the refusenik address list they brought with them from the United States, and over the next few hours visited refusenik apartments to dispense our gifts. The evening was emotionally satisfying, bringing some cheer to refusenik families, but anticlimactic compared to what I had lived through in Moscow. Each family we visited professed thanks for our visit, for the presents we brought, and served tea and whatever food they could spare.

The following day, we toured more of the city with a different guide and visited the palace and gardens of Peterhof. Often called the Russian Versailles, Petrodvorets (Peter's Palace) is grander than its French namesake. Peter the Great built this palace on a luxurious estate in the suburbs of the city beginning in 1714. Fountains and manicured gardens teeming with marble and gold statues filled the grounds and lined the walks. The Grand Cascade—sixty-four fountains and more than two hundred bronze statues dominated by Samson wrestling the jaws of a lion—glittered among the trees.

That afternoon, I packed my things and boarded a bus to the airport. My troubles began—again.

Samson wrestling the lion.

8

ESCAPE TO THE WEST

The customs agent wore a face that fit his angry demeanor: slits for eyes, unshaven beard, creased forehead, and pockmarked cheeks. He also smelled of a dribbled lunch and body odor.

He started with my gold wedding band. When I arrived in Moscow days earlier, I had to declare any valuables I brought with me. The Soviets kept tabs on what expensive items like jewelry came in and what went out. I had forgotten to list the ring.

"Where did you buy this ring?" he asked, his tone challenging.

"In the US, when I got married."

"No, you didn't. You didn't write it on the entry form, so you didn't have it when you entered the USSR."

"I just forgot to write it down."

The discussion was ludicrous. The agent and I both knew there was no place in the USSR where I could have bought such a gold ring. After squeezing me through a ringer, he let it go.

"What else did you forget to write down?"

"I think that's all."

"We'll see," he said. His eyes glittered in anticipation as they locked onto mine. "Empty your pockets."

A colleague, Jonathan Abrams from New Mexico, had waltzed through customs just before me and was waiting a few steps away. He asked the agent, "Why are you doing this? He's a VIP. Can't you see the label on his bag?"

The agent spit on the ground as he answered. *Ptui!* "VIP Moscow, not Saint Petersburg! Open everything!"

I had to empty the contents of my suitcase, then my briefcase, and finally my wallet. He had me turn my pockets inside out and patted me down to be sure they were empty. The line behind me lengthened and grew fidgety, but he ignored them. He fingered each item, held it to the overhead light for study, and carelessly flipped it back into my suitcase. I had a few rubles left in my wallet, and I thought he would steal them, but he didn't.

I had nothing to hide, but after Moscow, it was enough to make me break out in a cold sweat. I didn't know whether he knew anything about what I had done, or about last night's refusenik visits, or whether he was just angry at the VIP luggage tag. And I had no Chazov for protection.

Finally, after an agonizing ten minutes that seemed an eternity, the arrogant bastard let me go. I was trembling as Jonathan and I boarded the flight to Amsterdam, and I didn't stop shaking until we had cleared USSR airspace.

I called Joan right after we landed. It was a good thing I did. Frank Marcus had called her as soon as he landed, several days *before* her birthday. He told her he'd made it out safely with the film and was mailing it to me, and that when he left Moscow, I was still okay—as far as he knew—and I would try to call her on July 1.

"What in heaven's name are you talking about?" she had said to Frank.

She'd been waiting four days for me to call, frantic, imagining all sorts of horrors, until she heard my voice. I would have tried to call her from Moscow had I known. But calls were not easily placed and certainly would have been monitored by the KGB.

Frank mailed me the film. When I had it developed, incredibly the letter was so blurred—I had taken it hurriedly—it was illegible and could not be salvaged. All the emotional trauma I had experienced—for nothing!

I followed through on all the messages the refuseniks had given me. One call was very special: to Olga Plam, Naum's daughter living in Boulder, Colorado. She had been allowed to immigrate to the United States with her husband and son in 1976. The Soviets had refused Naum because he knew "state secrets" from nuclear work twenty-five years earlier. Olga was very concerned about her father's health. I reassured her that he was doing well.

Around that time, I became chairman of a committee in our temple focused on the plight of the refuseniks. The Indianapolis Jewish community was not generally aware of the problem. To highlight the issue, I suggested we call Naum in Moscow and have him address the congregation via a loudspeaker hooked to the phone so they could hear firsthand what he and other refuseniks were living through.

I was told it would be impossible to arrange—"No, you can't."

I wrote Naum and asked whether he would be able to accept a call from us in his apartment. He thought it might be possible since his phone was working again. He said the authorities would certainly listen in, and he couldn't predict what would follow. He was game to try. We arranged a time and a date several weeks hence.

I contacted Olga and invited her to spend a weekend with us in Indianapolis. I would pay her expenses. She eagerly accepted a chance to surprise her father on the phone.

Excitement was palpable as we prepared for the call. We had filled the temple, and everyone was buzzing about whether the call would go through. When the *brrrr* of the phone echoed on loudspeakers throughout the sanctuary, conversations stopped and we waited, breathing suspended.

Naum picked up at his end, and I could hear the happiness in his voice as we said hello and exchanged pleasantries. Then I put Olga on.

"Privet, Papa," Olga shouted. "Hello, Papa."

"Moya dorogaya doch!" Naum said. "My darling daughter!"

Oh my goodness! We couldn't understand a word because they were speaking Russian so fast, but we could hear the joy in their voices.

After three or four minutes, the line suddenly went dead.

Olga's face turned ashen. She held the receiver out to me with a helpless look, a silent plea to fix it.

With a constriction in my gut, we dialed again … and again, but the connection would not go through. We had no idea what had happened and imagined the worst: someone pulling the plug and the KGB storming the apartment to arrest Naum and Inna.

We found out later that the KGB had disconnected their phone but left Naum and Inna alone.

Russian cardiologists invited me back to Moscow to lecture a few years after my 1982 trip, but the government authorities refused to give me a visa. I checked with our local FBI for an explanation. They told me my name was on a blacklist.

"This is very bad," they told me. "Don't even consider going. You'll end up dead in a car accident or mugged in a dark alley."

9
FREEDOM FOR NAUM AND INNA MEIMAN

Naum contacted me in late 1985. Inna had a tumor in her neck inadequately treated after four surgeries by Moscow physicians. Could I help get her a visa to receive treatment in the United States?

Through the efforts of many people—I was a minor player—including the press, prominent rabbis, senators such as Ted Kennedy, and a hunger strike by Inna's close American friend, Lisa Paul, Inna got her visa in January 1987. The tumor had progressed, and she needed urgent care.

She flew to the United States and was admitted to Georgetown University Hospital for chemotherapy. I spoke with her by phone after she arrived. The travel and the initial medical evaluation had left her exhausted. I contacted the chief of medicine at Georgetown, a good friend named Charles Rackley, to check in on her and make certain they were doing everything possible to treat her cancer. Lisa Paul spent time with Inna, along with a few visitors. Before I had a chance to visit, Inna died.

The Soviet Union finally allowed Naum to leave for Israel in 1989. He came to the States for a series of university lectures and for a medical checkup I performed at Indiana. He stayed in our guest room.

A year or so after Naum returned to Tel Aviv, I visited him with a colleague, Robert Myerburg. Trying to recall the visit to Naum's apartment, I recently contacted Bob. He emailed: "I recall you putting a $100 bill in his book (on a bookshelf). You wanted to help him but didn't want to chance embarrassing him by handing it to him. I always wondered if he ever found it."

I don't know if he ever did. Naum died in Tel Aviv in March 2001.

In May 1999, after the collapse of the Soviet Union, I got another invitation to lecture in Moscow. The Russians—no longer the USSR—granted me a visa and let me back in. I was a little apprehensive but didn't think anything bad would happen to me in this new regime. Virtually all the refuseniks wanting to leave had left by then, and the trip was pleasant but uneventful.

VODKA CHALLENGE

10

In 1977, I made my first journey to the USSR, traveling as a representative of the National Heart, Lung, and Blood Institute. The NHLBI had established a US-USSR Cooperative Health Program on Cardiovascular Disease. Three of us—Bernard Lown, one of the leading cardiologists in the world at that time; Jack Titus, an outstanding cardiac pathologist from Texas; and I—traveled together over a three-week period to Moscow, Tbilisi (capital of Georgia), Vilnius (capital of Lithuania), and Kaunas (Lithuania's second largest city), lecturing and making friends with fellow cardiologists. We shared the latest scientific advances in the United States with our Soviet hosts who, in turn, lectured about the work they were doing.

Author and Bernard Lown, Moscow, 1977.

Lown was chair of our committee and had chosen the two of us to join him. Inviting Jack Titus was a no-brainer: Jack was an experienced pathologist, and much of the Soviet research interest centered on the pathology of sudden death. My selection as a heart rhythm expert was more of a surprise since, at the time, I was relatively unknown in the world of international cardiology.

Lown and I knew of each other through our medical publications, but we had met only at a scientific meeting some months before. I'd been nervous because Lown was an icon in clinical cardiology. People said his "golden tongue" never lost an argument. Lown could deliver acerbic commentary and rapid, lancinating ripostes that rendered opponents speechless and disarmed, reduced to stammering pretenders.

Before that meeting started, Lown introduced himself and said, "Someone told me you're nervous about being on the same program with me." He was shorter than I expected, with a broad forehead and receding brown hair. I was struck by his eyes—they seemed to flash intellect.

I nodded with an uneasy smile, unsure where his comments were going. "Yes, sir," I said.

He replied, "Well, I know you by reputation," he said, "and I'm equally nervous being on a panel with you."

I doubt he meant it—he seemed quite relaxed—but what a perfect response. We were respectful of each other's comments, and the interaction that followed was mutually satisfying. I suspect that influenced his decision to invite me on the USSR trip.

We started in Moscow, meeting with Chazov at the famed Myasnikov Institute of Cardiology, where he was director. Chazov, radiating charisma, introduced us to his staff, one of whom I'll call Dmitry, an electrophysiologist interested in our work.

Chazov suggested an exchange of scientists. Dmitry would spend three months in my lab in Indianapolis, and then I would send one of my young electrophysiologists to spend three months with Dmitry in Moscow. I readily agreed, knowing that the level of the commitment—Chazov in the USSR and the NHLBI in the United States—would make it easy to obtain the necessary papers, visas, and permissions.

My father had been born in Berditchev, a small shtetl outside Kiev, and immigrated to the United States in 1909 at age three. Since I had Russian—or at least Ukrainian—genes, I was excited to think I might be close to my family roots.

Raised on his mother's stories of pogroms, my father was concerned about my safety traveling to the USSR at the height of the Cold War. I didn't give it a second thought, but maybe I should have. I found out later that Dmitry's parents were similarly worried about his safety, a Russian traveling to the United States.

To match people and sites with the photos I took on that first trip, I'd brought a small recording device on this first trip to dictate the names of people I met and places I visited. I left it in my locked briefcase in the hotel room when we went out. As a fan of James Bond movies, I placed a strand of my hair on top of the device and carefully secured the lid of my briefcase.

After dinner the first night, I returned to my hotel room and unlocked the briefcase. The strand of hair was still in place, but someone had turned on the recorder and left it running. The battery—I had no replacement—was now dead, and so were my plans to document the trip by cassette. The Soviets must have been 007 fans too.

Doctors in all three cities met and hosted us. We held one- or two-day symposia at each stop, swapping scientific and medical information with our Russian colleagues. At the time, Soviet medicine lagged Western advances. We toured hospitals where ancient intravenous kits still used rubber tubing we had abandoned for disposable plastics years before.

The chief cardiologist in Tbilisi was a particularly charming and amiable host. He and Lown struck up a special camaraderie, and they sparred verbally during the day over politics, sports, whatever. At dinner that night, the chief cardiologist served as our host—a self-appointed *tamada*, or Russian toastmaster. He began the evening's dinner by taunting, "Tonight you drink as much as *you* want. Tomorrow night, you drink as much as *I* want."

He had laid down the gauntlet for a US-Soviet drinking contest.

This childish challenge astonished us. I hadn't engaged in a drinking contest since my fraternity days at Dartmouth. Lown confided he had never been part of one at all and was pretty much a teetotaler. Titus was a big guy and could probably hold his own. We agreed to play along as a courtesy and let the home team win in a rout.

The next day, the wily Georgian prepared a sightseeing tour of Tbilisi for us. He was particularly proud of Georgian brandy and the many distilleries in his city, some over a century old. He encouraged us to visit and sample the various cognacs at the tasting tables.

"We'd love to," I said. "You can show us the best ones."

"No," he replied, "I have work to do. I'll see you at dinner."

By late afternoon, we returned to our hotel tipsy from all our samplings. A short nap before dinner lowered our blood-alcohol levels a smidgen, but we still would not have passed a DUI test. Our host, working all day, was the picture of sobriety, I'm sure just as he planned.

When the dinner toasts began, the home team had us at a significant disadvantage.

After several vodka toasts, the tamada took note of my full glass. I had tried to sip instead of drink, but the glass's unchanging level was a dead giveaway.

The tamada stood and faced me.

"Dr. Zipes, you are the youngest member here, yet you are drinking the least. Not good."

He shook his head, stared me in the eye, and held his vodka glass aloft. "Dr. Zipes," he said in a loud voice, "I toast your wife and your children. Up your bottom!" The normal "bottoms up" salute thus transformed, he slugged down his vodka and turned the empty glass upside down on the table to underscore his feat.

Today, it seems easy to have declined the challenge. At that time and in that place, it was impossible. I downed my glass, and the spirited contest was on.

Unlike the United States hockey team that trounced the Russians in the 1980 Miracle on Ice, we succumbed easily to our Georgian challengers. By the end of dinner, we could barely stand. Someone had to help us to our rooms. I fell into an alcoholic stupor and didn't stir until someone pounded on my door for breakfast.

The tamada, proud of his victory, was magnanimous over hot tea the next morning. Perhaps our loss made a tiny contribution to Soviet détente—at least in Tbilisi.

Rather than compete for drinking prizes, our hosts in Vilnius, Lithuania, seemed more interested in physical fitness. When we arrived, they suggested we might want to relax with a refreshing sauna.

We sat for thirty minutes on wooden benches with towels draped across our laps, roasting in temperatures approaching 150 degrees Fahrenheit. An attendant poured cold water on hot coals, generating wet clouds of humid air that enveloped and almost suffocated us. We were soaked and couldn't distinguish dripping humidity from our own sweat. Standing made me light-headed. I had to grab the wall to steady myself as my blood pressure plummeted into heat-dilated blood vessels.

Attendants helped us into striped robes and pointed hats and herded us into an adjacent room. It felt like leaving equatorial Africa for the Arctic. Our hosts immediately dropped their robes and hats and plunged into a large ice-cold swimming pool. As with "up your bottom" in Tbilisi, we had no place to hide. When I hit the freezing water, those wide-open blood vessels contracted with such vehemence I think they stopped my heart. I fought sputtering to the surface before I could feel a heartbeat again. But we matched them stroke for stroke in the frigid pool, and our reward was—you guessed it—a vodka party.

Russian hosts at sauna, 1977. Author second from
left; Lown to author's left; Titus in back.

We left the pool with chattering teeth and hugged thick, white towels around our bodies, not to dry off but for warmth. Our hosts guided us into another room with a long table on which sat pitchers of vodka.

"It will drive out the chill," they said, swilling down large gulps of the fiery brew.

One of the cardiologists we met in Kaunas, Jonas Ragaisis, became my lifelong pen pal. Forty years later and well into his eighties, Jonas still writes to me about life in Kaunas and his retirement on a small pension. He sends me beautiful stamps and postcard pictures of his city.

I have reciprocated with cardiology textbooks and an occasional check. His most recent letter contained a picture taken during our meeting in 1977, showing a young Jonas, Lown, Titus, and me. Jonas has kept track of each of our letters. By his count, it was our 105th letter exchange.

*Jack Titus, Bernard Lown, Jonas Ragaisis, and author
(left to right)—Kaunas, Lithuania, 1977.*

11

THE BANQUET

The trip was so successful we soon returned to Moscow with our wives and NHLBI dignitaries. On this trip, we visited the ancient and exotic Uzbekistan cities of Tashkent (the capital), Bukhara, and Samarkand. Located in Central Asia on the timeworn Silk Road between China and the Mediterranean Sea, these three cities, thousands of years old, were once centers of learning, culture, religion, and trade. Each had distinctive mosques and madrasas (schools) decorated with intricate tile patterns in blues, greens, yellows, and reds. The muezzin (person appointed at a mosque to lead and recite the call to prayer) sounded a haunting mandate from tall, slender minarets attached to the mosques that reverberated over loudspeakers five times a day.

Central Asia in 1977 was a contrast of cultured and primitive living. In Tashkent, we enjoyed a production of Verdi's opera *Aida* sung in Russian at the local opera house. In Samarkand and Bukhara, the women complained that the toilets had no seats. Before they entered a stall, an LOL sitting on a wooden stool in the middle of the room doled out small squares of toilet paper she had just cut up, four pieces to each woman. In the street, locals repeatedly approached us to offer whatever they had in exchange for our jeans.

Yalta, our final city, was a luxurious contrast, a resort on the south coast of the Crimean Peninsula where yachts dotted the harbor of the Black Sea. However, our tourist hotel was still under construction after seven years. The hotel was situated on a wooded cliff with a spectacular view of the Black Sea. Parts of the building stodd as a bare-boned skeleton, anticipating more bricks and mortar in the future. Each room was still waiting for telephone installation.

On this second trip, Chazov met our plane at the Sheremetyevo Airport outside Moscow for a welcoming banquet. The sign on the wall alongside the dining room door read in English and Russian: *Room for Deputies of the Supreme Soviet.*

Joan, my wife, nudged me and pointed. "Very impressive," she whispered.

A tall, broad-shouldered man in a spotless uniform opened the door for us, and we entered. The room had nondescript beige wall coverings, a varnished oak floor, and three sparkling chandeliers that hung over a long banquet table. Place settings on a cream-colored tablecloth displayed precisely positioned, gleaming plates, glasses, and silverware.

Dinner was sumptuous, fueled by room-temperature vodka poured like water from pitchers in the center of the table. Each of the thirty-or-so guests was expected to offer a toast. The status of the guest determined the pecking order. Naturally, Chazov began, then turned to Lown, and so on down the line. After I gave mine, I warned Joan her time was coming.

When Joan's turn arrived, she panicked, stood, blurted out the only Russian phrase she remembered from studying Berlitz tapes, "Bo zheh moy!" ("Oh my God!"), and plunked back down, red-faced. The Russians howled with laughter.

After the laughter died down, she whispered, "Maybe the first happy howl ever in this august room."

That made me remember the sign. I had to have a picture of it. Between courses, I excused myself and left the room.

As I lined up my Polaroid Instamatic on that sign, I heard a growl behind me. "Nyet!"

I almost dropped my camera as a burly uniformed guard confronted me with a Kalashnikov automatic hanging from his shoulder. He waggled his finger, pointed at my camera with his gun, and shook his head.

I needed no Berlitz translation. Disappointed, I returned to finish dinner.

After the final toasts—praising our national leaders—were given, we all rose to leave. I asked Chazov and Lown if I could take their picture. Graciously they agreed, and I asked them to follow me. Outside the room, I positioned one on each side of the sign and snapped away. The guard glared but kept his automatic pointed at the floor and his mouth shut. I smiled, winked at him when I finished, and strolled away, safe under Chazov's protection.

Lown and Chazov with sign, 1977.

A RUSSIAN IN INDIANAPOLIS

12

Several months later, Dmitry became the first exchange scientist and one of the first Russians to visit our city. He was interested in our electrophysiology research and eager to begin experiments with us. He wanted to learn what equipment we used so he could replicate it in Moscow. Chazov had promised he would build him a lab like ours.

We were standing in the middle of Marsh, a large grocery store in Indianapolis, and Dmitry was paralyzed.

"I have never seen so much food in one place," he said, looking over my shoulder from the meat counter to the produce section. "How can you decide what to buy?"

With nicotine-stained fingers, he popped a Tums tablet into his mouth, an hourly routine for chronic heartburn. His eyes lit up as they focused on his first purchase: a supersized box of Tums. Antacids were often unavailable in Moscow, he said.

During the week, Dmitry stayed in an apartment NHLBI had rented for him near the university. On Fridays, he left work with me to become a weekend member of our family.

All things were new and exciting, like Marsh grocery and the TV in our guest bedroom where Naum had stayed. It was a small room on the first floor but had an adjacent private bath and was perfect for a short-term guest.

"Dmitry, want to try our lawn mower?" my sons asked in their best Tom Sawyer imitation during his first weekend with us. "It's a lot of fun."

Dmitry readily accepted and, having no shorts to wear in the hot summer sun, mowed the lawn in his boxer underwear. He was thrilled with the power mower and the exercise, as were my sons to unload a bothersome weekly summer chore. The neighbors soon buzzed about the Russian mowing the Zipes' lawn in his underwear. I bought Dmitry a pair of proper shorts, and mowing the lawn became his weekend project. We returned to work together on Monday morning, and he spent the rest of the week in his apartment.

After the first two months, Dmitry grew lonesome. He asked if he could call his wife in Moscow. He missed her and his two daughters. "I want to bring them jeans," he said. "They are quite valuable in Moscow, but I need to find out their sizes."

I gave him permission but asked him to keep the expensive, long-distance call short. He spoke for only five minutes, the happy, excited timbre in his voice showing how much he missed them. His eyes were moist toward the end of the call.

When he hung up, he looked at me with a sheepish grin. "Thanks," he said, "I got their measurements. Now both the KGB and the FBI know the sizes of my wife and daughters." He was probably right.

The exchange visit went well with only an occasional mishap. At dinner one Friday night, I splurged with wine. I asked Dmitry if he wanted any. "Yes," he said, "if you have fine white wine."

"It's pretty good," I said with a puzzled look on my face. "Medium priced. How fine did you want?"

"I just don't like sweet wine," Dmitry said.

I paused, considering his response until it dawned on me. "You mean *dry* white wine, not fine white wine."

He burst out laughing, the misunderstanding resolved.

The next mishap wasn't that easy to resolve and could have abruptly ended Dmitry's visit—perhaps even led to his arrest when he returned home.

Many of our neighbors were interested in our Russian houseguest, especially after the Tom Sawyer incident. Dmitry was a curiosity. The

United States wasn't exactly on friendly terms with the Soviets, with Jimmy Carter as president and Leonid Brezhnev the USSR general secretary. The Soviets were testing nuclear arms and were contemplating an Afghanistan invasion. International relations were strained.

I decided to have a neighborhood party to introduce our Russian houseguest to our friends.

Big mistake.

Dmitry insisted on being the tamada and shopped with me to be sure I bought lots of Stolichnaya vodka, eighty proof. Fifteen or so friends gathered on a Saturday evening in my living room, sitting on chairs, the sofa, or pillows placed on the floor. The living room was a few steps down from the kitchen and had sliding glass doors that opened to the backyard patio and garden. My neighbors chatted with Dmitry, asking about his family, life in Moscow, and how he liked the United States. Dmitry was very polite and a bit shy.

Then the toasts began, much like all my dinners in the USSR. As tamada, Dmitry led the way, shyness dissipated. I think he wanted to impress my neighbors. It was Tbilisi all over again.

What's with these Russians? I wondered. *Everything's a contest. Especially drinking.*

My next-door neighbor, Mickey Maurer, was not a big drinker. To still participate in the party and toasts, he filled his glass with spicy tomato juice, pretending to sip a Bloody Mary that was really a Virgin Mary. Whenever Dmitry came by with a vodka shot glass to refurbish his drink, Mickey accepted it and then poured the vodka into a large floor plant next to his chair when no one was looking. (The plant died two days later.)

What Mickey didn't know was that his lovely wife, Janie, sitting next to him, also a teetotaler, was pouring *her* vodka into *his* glass when *he* wasn't looking. He was actually drinking a stiff Bloody Mary and didn't know it. The spicy tomato juice camouflaged the taste of the alcohol.

After an hour or so, Mickey became quite drunk. "I don't feel too good," he said and left for home by the patio sliding doors. He held on to Janie for dear life and zigzagged across our lawn to his back door where, he told me the next day, he passed out in his bed.

Toward the end of the evening, conversation turned to our respective leaders and the animosity our countries shared. Dmitry was quite drunk and became belligerent as we each defended our country's leader and world position. I was sitting in a big easy chair near the fireplace when Dmitry sounded off in the middle of the room. I think he wanted to show my neighbors he was a staunch Soviet.

"Your President Jimmy Carter is a weak man," he said. "General Secretary Leonid Brezhnev is smarter and tougher. He will eat Carter for dinner—or maybe for breakfast." He raised a toast with his vodka glass. "I drink to that," he said.

He approached me and waved his finger in my face, balancing the vodka glass in his other hand. "Do you see these teeth?" he shouted, pointing to multiple silver caps in his mouth. "This was from starving during the war when the Nazis invaded Russia. I was just a kid."

He stood in front of my chair and leaned over me. He sneered an ugly smile to show his teeth. "You don't have metal caps like these, do you?" He touched my lips with his finger, and I thought he was going to force my mouth open.

I shoved his hand aside. "Stop this, Dmitry," I said. "You're drunk. It's time to end the party."

"Ha," he smirked. "You Americans think you're so tough. You are not. You are all too soft and too used to your luxuries."

He spun around, barely staying upright as his hand swept the room. "Look at this house. We could fit three or four families in here, not just one. You don't know how to sacrifice."

My neighbors were silent, standing or sitting in small groups, not knowing what to do. None were ready to confront the Russian. Several slipped out the front door. I was embarrassed that they had to hear his ranting.

Dmitry staggered against the side of my chair, bracing against it for stability. "You don't know how to fight either. Russians are a lot tougher. *When* World War III happens, we will bury you."

The last statement drew gasps from the remaining guests. I rose and pushed Dmitry away from my chair. I tried to take his vodka glass, but he waved it out of reach. I took hold of his arm, but he pulled away and stood in front of me in a belligerent boxer's stance.

One neighbor's twelve-year-old daughter gasped to her mother, "Oh my God. Dr. Zipes is going to get into a fist fight with that Russian."

I don't know if Dmitry overheard her or the buzzing from the other remaining guests, but he looked around and suddenly seemed to become aware of the situation. He lurched to the sliding doors and stumbled into the garden, across the lawn, and on into the night, glass clutched tightly in hand. He knew nothing about the neighborhood, and I wasn't certain he'd find his way back. But it was past eleven at that point, and I didn't much care.

My heart was thumping fast, and I took a moment to collect myself.

I turned to the remaining guests. "Thanks, everybody, for coming, but I think the party's over."

"You going to be okay?" one neighbor asked, a burly guy who'd been a college football player many years before. His fists flexed in concern. "I can stay if you need help."

"I'll be fine, but thanks for asking." I didn't think Dmitry would be violent, but my hands were trembling.

The guests trickled out, some shaking their heads and mumbling. "That's why there'll never be peace between our countries. You can't trust the bastards." I shut the door behind them.

"What're you going to do?" Joan asked as we cleaned up. "He might get lost. Maybe you should go look for him."

I shook my head. "He picked this fight."

"But he was drunk."

"That's when the truth comes out. He made his bed—"

"He may not have one if he gets lost," she said.

"That's his problem. We're going to ours. I'll leave the patio doors unlocked. He can find his way back—or not. The night's warm if he ends up outside." I started up the stairs to our bedroom. "Coming?"

I waited. She looked out the glass doors into the empty night and then followed me up the stairs.

We were up early Sunday morning. Joan was preparing breakfast when Dmitry slunk from the guest bedroom, looking haggard. He made his way to the kitchen holding his head with both hands. "Too much vodka last night," he said, sitting down at the kitchen table. "Could I have some black coffee, please?"

That was the end of the discussion. Neither of us ever mentioned the incident. I think he was too scared to bring it up. Without discussing what had happened, we could pretend it didn't exist. Maybe he thought I was too drunk to remember. Maybe he was. He knew one word from me to our government or to Chazov could wreck his career.

Our interactions continued, uncomfortable and strained. The rest of the month was chilly, focused entirely on science. I stopped bringing him home on weekends, and he left for Moscow at the end of the month.

Dmitry went on to have a successful career as a heart rhythm scientist in Moscow.

REUNION WITH EVGENY CHAZOV

My last Russian encounter was an unexpected but happy reunion with my friend Evgeny Chazov. In 1985, he had been awarded the Nobel Peace Prize, shared with Bernard Lown, for forming the International Physicians for the Prevention of Nuclear War.

In 2013, the European Society of Cardiology bestowed its highest award, a gold medal for contributions to cardiology, on both Chazov and me at their annual scientific meeting in Amsterdam, Netherlands. We shared the stage in a wonderful ceremony that highlighted our work in front of several thousand people.

Irina (daughter), Evgeny Chazov, author, and Joan
at ESC Gold Medal Ceremony, 2013.

Evgeny was as warm and friendly as he had been when we first met almost forty years before. We were both thrilled to receive this honor and to share it with each other. His English had become a bit rusty, and he used his charming daughter Irina as his interpreter.

"Do you remember the dinner you hosted for us at the Sheremetyevo Airport?" I asked him.

Evgeny nodded. "Da."

I recounted the story of taking his and Lown's picture in front of the impressive room sign. He laughed delightedly and clapped me on the back.

Though tempted, I did not bring up the refusenik incident. Neither did he.

PART II

THE EARLY YEARS

14

BIG GUY

I have often thought about my reaction to people telling me no and wondered where and when my contrary nature began. It might have been when I crossed paths with Big Guy.

My father gave me a Daisy Red Ryder pump action BB gun for my eighth birthday. Guns were quite acceptable when I was growing up. As kids, we went to the movies every Saturday afternoon to see Westerns featuring cowboys shooting Indians. Roy Rogers, Gene Autry, Hopalong Cassidy, and the Lone Ranger could shoot the gun from the hand of a bad guy at twenty yards while bouncing in the saddle of a horse running at full gallop.

I practiced shooting in our small backyard, plinking at old tin cans, bottles (fun to see them explode, but then I had to pick up all the shards), and an occasional rat dumb enough to venture out in daylight. Practice over, I'd hunt spent BBs (a big drain on my paper route income), clean and reuse them. After a year, I was deadly at thirty feet, even with moving targets.

One of the resident rodents I shot at decided to change homes and found a way indoors. He was a big gray rat that flitted around our attic, leaving a trail of destruction. No box was safe from his incisors. When he honed his teeth on Mom's suitcase and soiled her wedding dress, she ordered, "Death to the invader."

Easier said than executed.

Big Guy made the attic his vacation home. Impervious to rattraps and rat poison, BG either ignored them or was too tough to kill. We'd find the trap sprung—but no BG; the poison-laced bait gone—but no BG. Like the drug kingpin El Chapo, BG had a secret tunnel to exit and enter. Though he left droppings all over, I couldn't find his escape hatch.

The attic was small. You could stand erect only in the very center, where the slanted, unfinished wooden beams joined to create the ceiling peak. From there the beams sloped downward on each side for ten or twelve feet, meeting the floor like a V on its side. Planks of raw wood formed the walls. Except for what light came through a tiny window on the outside wall, the attic was dark, dank, and cobwebbed, emitting musty odors that gave me chills. I knew BG lurked somewhere, even if I couldn't see him. I had to muster all my courage to enter, especially at night. We always kept the door bolted shut.

One day I came home for lunch—Roselle Avenue Elementary School was a ten-minute walk from my house—to find my mother all excited.

"We caught BG! Dead as a doornail," she said, "lying next to the rat trap in the attic. Sentence carried out." She pounded her fist on the table like a judge's gavel.

I charged up the stairs to see for myself. There he was, lying alongside the sprung trap. Victory at last. BG vanquished.

Not.

His tail twitched, and his chest moved. Just stunned, probably suffering post-traumatic conscussion. We should have named him Super Rat.

"Mom," I shouted, "BG's still alive. Call Dad." My father's auto shop was a few blocks from home, and he would be returning for lunch.

"I did already," she said. "He's busy with a customer. He'll come when he can."

"What should I do?" I asked.

Wrong.

A nine-year-old boy should never ask his mother what to do in a situation like this. I should just have gotten my Red Ryder, held it to BG's head, and filled his skull with BBs. My trigger finger itched to do it. "Ask forgiveness, not permission" was a fundamental precept I'd yet to learn, a particularly important lesson when faced with "No, you can't."

"Turn the wastebasket on top of him, and Dad will dispose of him when he comes home," she said.

I did as I was told, wolfed down my peanut butter and jelly sandwich, drank a glass of milk, and returned to fourth grade sucking on an all-sour pickle, my favorite. We picked them out of big wooden pickle barrels for five cents each on Bathgate Avenue in the Bronx. (The only place I can get the same pickles today is in New York City. I order a gallon of them from The Pickle Guys about every other month. They send it Federal Express, which costs more than the price of the pickles!)

Three hours later, I raced home from school, straight to the attic. Very slowly I lifted the basket.

No BG.

"What happened?" I asked my mother.

"When Dad got home, the rat was gone. He escaped like Houdini."

"Should I reset the trap?" I asked.

"Yes," Mother said. "I want that rat gone for good."

It was now four thirty on a snowy winter's day in Westchester County, New York. That meant the sun was pretty much gone. Snow flurries blanketed the windows. And that meant the attic would be almost dark. I wasn't happy about opening that door to set the trap. I had rebaited it with peanut butter—no jelly—and could picture BG getting a whiff and licking his lips at dinner being served.

I swallowed my fear and did as Mother asked. Opening the door to the attic very deliberately, I poked my head in. "You in there, BG?" I asked loudly. No answer. Braver, I put a foot into the attic and peered around. "Hey, Super Rat, you here?"

I heard a rustling in the far reaches of the attic, at the very point where the dipping roof met the floorboards. In the dying light from the snow-covered window, a pair of beady red eyes glared at me. It was too dark to see his body, but this had to be the resurrected BG, the Lazarus Rodent.

And I'm unarmed, I thought.

I dropped the rattrap—the released crossbar hit the wood with a loud *snap*—and dashed out. "Dinner's on me," I shouted to BG as I slammed the door. I stood still for a moment and caught my breath. I went to my room and grabbed Red Ryder. I had to finish this once and for all.

I ran downstairs. "Hey, Mom."

"What?" She was in the tiny kitchen preparing dinner, a red apron tied around her waist. The concentrated look on her face indicated she was in no mood for rat talk.

Nana, my mother's mother, sat at the kitchen table slicing carrots and celery for the salad. The appetizing aroma of fresh veggies filled the room. We ate at the stroke of six every night, come hell or high water. The previous summer, it had been my turn at bat with bases loaded, last inning, a Good Humor ice pop at stake, and I had to leave for dinner. Being late was not an option.

"I found him," I said.

"Hmm," she said.

"No, really, it's BG. We have to get him."

"Hmm."

"Mom, this is serious." I tugged her dress. "I want to kill him."

"With what? He's got more lives than a cat," she said without looking up.

"My Red Ryder," I said, holding the rifle aloft.

She frowned. Nine-year-olds didn't talk about killing. A rattrap or poison was one thing—it was impersonal, like a tornado or a lightning strike. Shooting was in another league, a much more intimate one. Your finger pulled the trigger, so you were the direct cause of the death. I had read someplace that one gun in a firing squad was always loaded with blanks so the shooters didn't know who actually pulled the trigger that killed the guy.

Finally, I had her attention. She stopped peeling potatoes and turned to me, her hands still twitching in a peeling motion. Her brain had shifted to a new topic but apparently hadn't told her hands. Nana suspended hers over the salad bowl.

"You're serious," Mom said, looking me in the eyes.

"Absolutely," I said. "He's in the eaves of the attic, and I can shoot him. He's got no place to run."

"Point that thing at the floor," she said, pushing my gun arm down. I complied.

"No, you can't," she said.

Even at age nine, I bristled. "Why not?"

"Because I said so. No killing like that."

"But *why?*" I was already regretting asking for permission.

"Because." She looked at the clock. "Because it will be time for dinner soon."

"That's no reason."

"Because the rat will bleed on the rug," she said.

"Mom," I said, unable to keep exasperation from my voice, "it's in the attic. Who cares? Besides, there's no rug." I wouldn't take no for an answer.

She sighed, resigned. "Okay, then, go ahead," she said, "but don't be late for dinner." She started peeling again, her hands moving faster than before to make up for lost time. My mother was very efficient. She shopped at the local A&P, knew the exact aisle for every item, and was in and out in, like, three minutes with food enough for the week.

"I can't do it alone. It's too dark. I need you to come with me and hold the flashlight." I didn't add that, given my druthers, I'd rather have had my father, but this couldn't wait.

She didn't move—bemused or confused, I couldn't tell.

"Mom," I said, looking at the clock. "It's only five o'clock; we've plenty of time before dinner. This'll only take five minutes, ten tops. But I need your help. If we don't do it now, BG'll disappear again, and we'll have to start all over with the traps and bait. I have to shoot him now. Next time he'll probably chew a hole in your wedding dress, not just dirty it." I didn't know if that was true, but it seemed like a good argument. I had a lot to learn about women, but I figured a wedding dress was something sacred that had to be protected.

Mother tossed me a dubious look, but I could see my last comment hit home. She hated guns and got mad at my father when he brought home the Red Ryder. He was now talking about a Mossberg .22 rifle for my next birthday. "A real gun that shoots real bullets for a ten-year-old? Are you out of your mind?" was her response.

"Mom, you want a big old rat living in your house?" I turned to my grandmother for support. "What about you, Nana? You go to bed at night listening to BG scratching next door. Isn't that scary?"

Nana shook her head, setting her gray bun waggling. "No," Nana said. "He doesn't make any noise—leastwise, I can't hear any." Nana was pretty deaf. "And as long as the attic door's shut, he can't bother me, and I sure won't open it to bother him."

No help from this source. Nana was a tough old bird, and a rat living in the attic adjacent to her room didn't faze her. A month earlier, on a shopping trip to New York City with my mother, some guy had tried to rip off her pocketbook in broad daylight on Fifth Avenue. She held on and beat him over the head with her umbrella until the cops came to arrest him. You didn't mess with Nana.

"Where's the flashlight?" my mother asked, lips pressed tight and the corners of her mouth downturned. "Let's make this quick." She dried her hands on her apron. "I don't like doing it one bit." She exhaled a loud huff. "Not one bit."

Before she could change her mind, I ran to the hall closet and grabbed the flashlight. "Let's go," I said. I couldn't keep the eagerness from my voice—mixed with a bit of fear. What an adventure. Teddy Roosevelt staring down a charging rhino in the Serengeti Plain had nothing on me.

My mother followed me upstairs, her footsteps lagging. I opened the door to the attic, flipped on the flashlight, stooped low, and walked in. Mother was right behind, her hand on my shoulder, perhaps for my restraint but most likely for her reassurance—maybe mine as well.

I played the beam along the eaves. There he was. BG crouched low against a wooden beam, shrinking from the light. His fierce red eyes glinted at us. I don't know if rats feel emotion, but to me those eyes seemed filled with hate.

I heard my mother gasp. "God, he's big—and scary."

I patted her shoulder and handed her the flashlight, keeping the beam trained on the rat. Her hand shook, and the beam bounced.

"Hold it steady, Mom. Use two hands if you have to. I can't shoot if I can't see him."

"You sure you want to do this? Suppose you miss?" Her voice was as shaky as her hands.

"I won't miss. Just keep the light trained on him."

"I don't think I can do this. Let's wait for your father."

"BG'll be gone by then. We have to do this now," I said.

"Well, be quick. I have to make dinner," she said between chattering teeth.

Dinner was the last thing on my mind. We were facing a mad, destructive rat in a dark room, and I was about to make my first kill. History books years from now would record this momentous event in my life.

I took aim with my Red Ryder. "Steady, Mom. You're shaking too much. The beam is—"

In a flash, BG was gone!

"Oh my God," Mom gasped. "Where'd he go?"

"Give me the flashlight," I said. "Hold the rifle for a minute." I could picture her look of revulsion as we swapped flashlight for gun.

I played the light around. There he was. He'd moved about ten feet, still lurking in the eaves, still staring with those malevolent red eyes. He wasn't going to pose long.

"Mom, this is the last chance." I gave her the flashlight and took the gun. "Hold the beam steady. Give me a shot."

I think fear paralyzed her, because she froze in place. I could see BG clearly. I took aim just behind his shoulder, where I pictured his heart beating four or five hundred times a minute. I'd read in *National Geographic* that rodents had very fast heart rates.

Pow!

The BB found its mark, but BG barely stirred. In fact, he twitched his shoulder like he might at an annoying fly. I envisioned the tiny round BB ricocheting like a bullet off armor plate.

"Keep steady, Mom." I lined him up again in my sights.

Pow!

Same shot, same response.

Mom dropped her hands. "I've had it. I'm leaving. I need to make dinner." She had a new tone in her voice, a catch in her throat. I could tell she didn't like this, but I didn't know if she was scared, felt this was cruel, or what. Making dinner was probably the least of it.

"Okay," I said, guiding her hands back to shine the light on BG. "One more shot. I'll finish him off."

I aimed for his head this time, right between those glowering red eyes.

Kapow!

BG shook his head. The inflamed reds seemed to grow bigger, angrier, and they fixed directly on me. I swear he snarled, and his teeth appeared enormous.

Suddenly, BG had had enough. He charged right at us!

"Aaaaiiiieeee!" Mom screamed. She dropped the flashlight and tore out of the attic so fast I felt the breeze as she left. Her primal instinct for self-preservation trumped any feelings of mother love or protection of her young.

I stood alone in the pitch-black room holding my Red Ryder pump action BB gun, facing the murderous onslaught of one demonic, red-eyed, pissed-off rat. My heart rate rivaled his, and my heart pumped as if it wanted to burst.

I fumbled for the errant light, the beam still shining. I seemed to move in slow motion, but it took just an instant. BG's nails scratched the floorboards as he raced toward me. I imagined those menacing eyes staring into mine as he attacked, his nails digging into my neck, his teeth tearing into my cheek. BG's bristles flicked my hand as I grabbed for the light.

But BG must have been as frightened as I, with only escape in mind. That headshot had to hurt. He ripped past me, and I whirled to follow his retreat. My beam caught him diving through a hole in the floor, his escape tunnel.

I collapsed to my knees. My hands were shaking so much I couldn't grip the BB gun, and it fell alongside me. I closed my eyes and buried my face in my hands. A nine-year-old boy didn't cry, but I was so frightened I was on the verge. I stayed that way a full five minutes until my breathing slowed and my heart stopped its crazy thumping. I listened for BG's scratching, but the attic was dead quiet. After a while, I stood on wobbly legs, collected Red Ryder, and left, locking the attic door behind me.

At dinner, my mother told my father a somewhat different tale of heroism, but I didn't bother to correct her. Mission accomplished— well, almost. I did want that kill, but maybe it was better this way. I wondered how Teddy Roosevelt felt after he murdered all those wild African animals.

After dinner, with my father holding the flashlight, I boarded up the hole in the attic. That was the last we saw of BG.

15

WORKING

Though Pleasantville was a rather wealthy town in Westchester County, New York, lots of blue-collar families had fathers who pumped gas, unstopped toilets, and repaired roads. We were one of them. My father put in long hours running a Texaco gas station. After he and his brother sold it, my father retailed tools for a while and then opened an auto repair shop in a small building at the back of a coal yard rented from a friend.

Summers at the repair shop (the place was so ugly it deserved no distinctive name, so we called it simply The Place) were blistering hot, with just a single fan pushing hot air around. In the winter, we froze our butts off as a tiny coal stove struggled to warm our icy fingers and toes.

Growing up in my family was as Dickens wrote in *A Tale of Two Cities*: "It was the best of times, it was the worst of times." Discipline was strict. Mother's mantra echoed off the walls: "Just wait until your father comes home."

Author, age one.

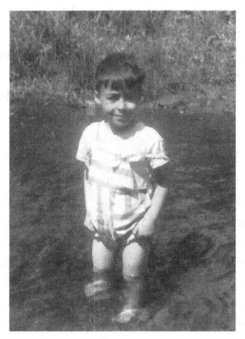

Author, age six.

My shenanigans often generated a list of punishments my father hung from the kitchen light cord before he left for work in the morning. A wet shoe from a slip on the muddy creek bank near the house sent me to bed right after dinner. Sassy talk got me grounded. Rarely his strap put a few smart ones across my bottom. I must have been particularly bad the year I received coal in my Christmas stocking.

At times, fate also conspired against me. A car backing down a slippery, snow-covered driveway flattened my brand-new Flexible Flyer sled on its first outing. After a fight at school while wearing the Boy Scout uniform I'd just bought with allowance saved for a year, I rubbed off grass stains with a sponge grabbed from the kitchen sink that had been previously soaking in bleach. I realized too late my first baseball glove, again purchased from precious savings, was a softball mitt. I had to pad my hand with a folded handkerchief to catch a baseball.

The family work ethic was strong, but mortgage payments were precarious on the erratic income from my father's auto repair shop and my mother's typing. Before we could afford a television, my father and I would watch the Friday Night Fights at Bleckner's Furniture Store. George Bleckner was a family friend who sold TVs. I used to babysit his son for twenty-five cents an hour. Three hours was a big night.

When I was eight, my father built a little wooden wagon that I wheeled on summer days near the train station to peddle jewelry cast off by female family members. I made eleven dollars that first summer, working eight-hour days.

I began caddying at the local golf course, Briar Hall Country Club, when I was eleven (I told the caddy master I was twelve). Toting bags at the rich man's club sucked in general—"yes, sir, no, sir" was not my cup of tea—but caddying for women was a challenge. Most of them played poorly and tipped even worse. A ball hit in the woods? My God, you'd think it was made of gold. And if they had a call of nature, they'd take a lifetime finding a suitable bush. "Close your eyes," they'd shout, squatting. After, they'd ask, "Where can I wash my hands?" Like I carried soap and water in my pockets.

Author as caddy with unidentified golfer, 1954.

The most sought-after golfers were the few men who tipped two bucks instead of the usual one. The owner of the Briar Hall Country Club (which became the Trump National Golf Club Westchester in 2001)—I think his name was Henry Smith—was a great bag to get. I knew his game and always had the right club ready. He hit his trusty eight-iron for all pitch-and-run approach shots. When he hit into the woods, he always had a good lie and a clear path to the green. Once, he gave me a dozen new golf balls when he won a match against another member. Their usual stakes were a lot higher than golf balls. I often watched my entire year's college expenses change hands on the eighteenth green.

My father was a dreamer with get-rich-quick schemes—he would invent something or compose a song that would sell millions. His invention was to facilitate cast removal. He envisioned burying a wire in the plaster of Paris at the time the cast was wrapped around a broken arm or leg. Pulling the wire would split the cast apart like opening an envelope. The idea went nowhere.

He called the song "Holes in My Shoes." It was about some guy who's happy even though he's poor and sings about it. The song never sold.

A personal experience cured me of any dreams of instant success. While I was caddying one Sunday, word spread from the caddy master, a horse track veteran, that the winner for the trotters in the third race at Yonkers Raceway the following Monday was fixed. Hanover's Darling would pay ten-to-one.

My usual take for the entire summer caddying was $600 or $700. If I could bet $50 or $60, I could retire until next year. But who had that kind of cash? Club members. One of them loaned it to me.

It turned out the whole race was rigged. Hanover's Darling broke stride midway through the race and finished dead last. I caddied for that member most of the summer to avoid personal bankruptcy.

I attended Pleasantville High School where I was an okay athlete but a pretty good student, especially in science and math. I played drums in the high school orchestra and band, and delivered newspapers after school.

I also marched in a band hired by the BPOE, Benevolent and Protective Order of Elks, a men's club, some Saturday afternoons after I finished caddying. We got five bucks for parading five miles while playing Sousa marches. BPOE even hired cheerleaders to strut out front.

That was where I met my first love, Marion, a slightly chunky, buxom redhead from a great Italian family. Her father ran a pizza shop, and her mother taught us how to cha-cha. She would put on a recording of "Tea for Two" or "La Bamba," and we would practice dancing in her kitchen. "One, two, cha, cha, cha." They were very religious Catholics, and Marion would cross herself each time we drove past a Catholic church. Marion and I dated until I left for college. Parting broke both our teenage hearts, but we soon recovered.

A member of the country club gave me a used set of clubs when I first started caddying. I polished the rust off and glued on new grips. I never had a sand wedge but used the pitching wedge for traps. I found a pair of cast-off golf shoes two sizes too big, stuffed the toes with paper, and buffed them as best I could. Golf balls came from the woods along the golf course, or I waded in the lake to retrieve them. Sometimes the head greenkeeper would let caddies play Mondays when the club was closed. I learned to play by reading paperbacks by Ben Hogan and Arnold Palmer. I got pretty good, played on the high school golf team, and had a hole in one when I was seventeen.

I can still picture the hole sixty-one years later, as distinct as a sharp PowerPoint slide. It was 173 yards long, all carry to an elevated green, with a steep drop-off into woods on the right and a large trap on the left. I hit a four iron and watched the ball fly straight toward the flag. The tee was too low to see the green, but a guy sitting on a tractor mowing the fairway behind us suddenly screamed, "Holy shit! It went into the hole. You got yourself a hole in one, kid."

Fortunately, it was James Baird Golf Course, a public golf course, so I didn't have to buy drinks for the house, just my playing partner, Sam Trapazzo. Trapper, like a lot of fathers of my friends at the time, caddied mornings at Briar Hall before working a second job. We'd become good buddies, and we often played golf together on Monday mornings, which was Caddy's Day.

Scooping that Titleist out of the hole and jotting a 1 on the scorecard was a huge thrill. I mailed the ball to the company, and they mounted it on a red tee in the center of a green felt background surrounded by brass. I still have that trophy somewhere.

When I was a junior in high school, I entered a county-wide caddy tournament held on a golf course in Westchester County—Winged

Foot, I think. A small gallery (mostly parents—mine were working) surrounded the first tee when we started and the eighteenth green as we finished. Though nervous, I hit a great tee shot that split the fairway on that first hole and almost holed my wedge from a deep sand trap at the eighteenth green.

Amazing that I still remember those two shots. Jon Voight, whose father was a golf pro and who would become the father of Angelina Jolie almost twenty years later, won the tournament. I placed third, which led to my very first airplane ride to the regionals in Michigan, where I choked and shot eighty.

As the only son—I have an older and a younger sister—I received a lot of attention because I was to be the family's salvation. My achievements would win back family respect, lost by my father to his two younger, more financially successful brothers.

How would I accomplish all this? "Become a doctor," my father said. "Be your own boss." Money and family standing would follow. Fortunately, that meshed with my own desires but for different reasons. I liked biology and science; I liked problem solving; and I liked helping people. No-brainer. Medicine was perfect. I would become a doctor but for my reasons, not his.

The high school guidance counselor had other ideas. When I asked her for advice about the path to medicine, she basically said, "No, you can't." After all, I was from a working-class family and had little money. Blue-collar kids didn't become doctors. She thought at the very least I should learn automobile mechanics as a backup.

I did help my father at The Place winter weekends when I wasn't caddying. I learned how to replace shock absorbers and brake pads, align and balance wheels, and set spark plug timing.

I knew it wasn't my thing. I hated The Place and resented working there, even before I damn near killed myself twice.

The first time, I was backing a car off an elevated ramp after changing the brake pads. I didn't realize someone had moved one of the two parallel metal tracks leading from the floor to the ramp. As I backed the car, I suddenly heard my father yell, "Doug, stop!" I jammed on the brakes just in time. The right rear wheel was suspended over ten feet of empty space, and the car was teetering, about to roll onto its side. I got enough traction on the left tire to drive back onto the ramp. But it was close.

The second time was when I was changing shock absorbers. My father had gone to get a new set from an auto supply shop and I thought I'd surprise him by having the car ready by the time he returned. I had the automatic wrench whirring off the old bolts on the right front shock when I heard my father once again shout, "Doug, stop!" He had just returned and saw I had forgotten to put a jack under the shock before taking it off. The shock absorber was a few threads away from springing loose and jackknifing into my face.

My father also nearly died when a jack slipped with him under a car. He managed to hold up a big Cadillac with his chest until help arrived, "only" suffering a bunch of broken ribs.

Once, a man asked me to wash and simonize his car by hand for fifteen dollars. That took four hours of hard scrubbing, but it was a lot of money. When I finished, my father said I had to pay him part of the fee because I had used his garage. An appeal to our family's supreme court (my mother) overruled his request.

As if these incidents weren't enough to convince me I would never follow his footsteps, an event seared forever in my brain did.

It was 1954, Christmas vacation when I was fifteen. I was home writing a book report on Conrad's *Heart of Darkness* (a boring read at the time) when my mother called from her secretarial office at the *Reader's Digest*. Westchester County was in the middle of a blizzard, and many *Digest* editors were stuck in the parking lot. Would I help my father put chains on their cars? We could make five bucks a car.

It wasn't a request, not if I wanted dinner that night. I donned parka and boots and trudged four blocks to my father's garage. The temperature was an icy fifteen degrees, with biting, gusting winds blowing snow into six-foot drifts. The pewter sky forecast a tenacious storm. Auto traffic had all but stopped, and the streets were empty. By the time I arrived at The Place, my eyebrows were frozen, and I couldn't feel my nose, ears, or fingertips.

Putting chains on a car is a daunting task in ugly weather with a foot of snow on the ground and fingers stiff with cold. It took us almost half an hour working together to wrap spiked chains on the rear wheels of our family Buick. Despite the freezing temperature, we were drenched in sweat and covered in snow. But I did learn something useful. Now, whenever it snows and I can't get in touch with AAA or call Uber, I know how to put chains on my car—if I had them.

Finally finished, we drove two miles at about twenty miles an hour to the *Reader's Digest* in Chappaqua. The road was a whiteout, and a bunch of cars had skidded into the ditch alongside.

My mother met us at the entrance to the *Reader's Digest* main building, a three-story redbrick edifice with a tall, white, central spire that made it look like a church. DeWitt and Lila Acheson Wallace, owners of the *Digest*, were caring, religious people. In fact, years later, after the birth of our first child, I received a handwritten congratulatory note from them.

Mother guided us to the editorial office. The warmth of the brightly lit interior hallway started to thaw my frozen bones.

We paused at the doorway to a large room, and I looked out at the editorial staff sitting at their desks, typing away. At least a dozen men and women were all warm and dry and dressed immaculately in jackets and ties, white shirts, blouses and skirts.

My father and I stood awkwardly at the threshold, dripping in grimy overalls, muddy boots, and black knit caps pulled low over our ears. We were going to slog into that blizzard for five bucks a car while the editors remained warm and cozy at their typewriters.

I was overcome with embarrassment and shame. I shouldn't have felt that way. After all, we were just a hardworking father and son ready to provide a service and make an honest dollar. But that was how I felt. I looked at them, and I looked at us, and I silently vowed, *Never will this ever happen to me again. The fires of hell won't prevent me from becoming a doctor.*

16

JOAN JACOBUS

Over the next three years, I worked even harder in high school and graduated in 1957 second in my class.

"You want to what—apply to Ivy League schools? You'd better have some community college backups," the counselor said.

Damn the naysayers. I was accepted by each college or university to which I applied, including the Ivy League schools. My first choice was Dartmouth College. I fell in love with it at first sight. Plus, they offered me a full tuition scholarship. I even received a small scholarship from the *Reader's Digest*.

My life as an adult began at Dartmouth. No one in my family had gone to college, so I had no one for guidance. I made all my own decisions and learned to live with the consequences. I worked after classes, as my high school counselor had predicted, but I quit when it interfered with my studies.

Freshmen at Dartmouth could not pledge fraternities (Dartmouth was all male at the time). When the sophomore brothers at one fraternity house planned a three-hour road trip to Skidmore College (all girls) and offered to take me along, I jumped at the chance. I hadn't even *seen* a woman in two months. Such "dirty rushing" was a no-no, but when they proposed to fix me up with a blind date, I said, "Screw the rules," and barreled into the car.

Joan Jacobus was her name. Cute, petite, dark haired with a

vivacious personality, we hit it off from the first minute. I was wearing my one new sports coat and looked pretty dapper. Since I was with the fraternity brothers, I assumed they told her I was one of them, a sophomore among sophomores.

We went to some sort of a disco in Saratoga Springs. I was now a cha-cha expert.

"How do you like Dartmouth?" she asked while we were dancing.

"Super school. I love my classes. Last year as a freshman, we had to read the Dartmouth Bible. I thought that was pretty neat."

"And the fraternity?" she asked.

"Great brothers at TEP. I share a room with four other guys, but it's not bad. We have lots of parties, mostly with the townies. You know, Dartmouth is just guys."

I answered all Joan's questions about classes I was taking and life at the fraternity with pure, fabricated sophomore fantasy.

Toward the end of a delightful evening, she sprang the trap.

"Are you ready to confess?" she asked.

I could feel my face redden. "What do you mean?" I blustered.

"About being a sophomore?" She had known all along I was a freshman and had let me go on and on with my unadulterated bullshit about sophomore life at Dartmouth.

What could I say? When you find yourself in a hole, stop digging. I apologized, came clean as a freshman, and we dated for the next three years.

I had very little money to spare after buying books and food and paying for laundry. When Joan visited Dartmouth for a weekend like Winter Carnival, I smuggled her into a dorm room vacated by a friend to avoid the cost of putting her up in the Hanover Inn. They charged five bucks a night, crowding twenty or thirty girls into rooms jam-packed with bunk beds.

Having women in Dartmouth dorms was an infraction that could have gotten me expelled. But I chanced it to save the money.

One morning, Joan woke to a janitor sweeping the floor and emptying the wastebasket in my friend's room. She burrowed her head beneath the blankets. He either didn't see her or was a good guy because he didn't report it.

Toward the end of three years of dating, our relationship heated up, and we decided to get married.

"No, you can't," my father decreed. "You're still in school, she'll get pregnant, your grades will drop, and you'll have to quit to support a family. Wait until you finish school. You can't get married now."

Even Joan's parents were not very happy, especially her mother. "Marry a struggling medical student," her mother said, shaking her head, "and you'll have to eat dark meat tuna fish for a long time. And if he goes into research, you'll probably starve."

No way were we going to wait.

Dartmouth College offered the opportunity for some students to enroll in Dartmouth Medical School after just three years as an undergraduate. I was fortunate to be accepted. Halfway through my first year of medical school, Joan and I got married in Rollins Chapel on the Dartmouth campus.

"She must be pregnant," my parents concluded. They discussed boycotting the wedding but eventually relented, driving the six hours from Pleasantville to Hanover with my sisters.

Our wedding day was cold, rainy, and gloomy outside as well as in. My parents, especially my father, were sullen and angry. I had disobeyed his direct order not to get married. How dare I defy him when he was only doing it for my own good?

Parents often get it wrong—mine did. Each of Joan's and my siblings, married under ideal circumstances with parental blessings, have divorced at least once and remarried. Ours is the only first marriage that lasted, fifty-six years at the time of this writing. I've often wondered why. I think it's because, as we grew older, we grew together, continuing to satisfy each other's needs and desires as they changed. Great sex helps!

Author and wife, Joan, at her most recent birthday.

Joan kept us solvent after the marriage, working as a secretary for the dean of Thayer School of Engineering at Dartmouth.

The choices of places to live for a married couple in the middle of the school year were not vast in a small college town like Hanover. I found two options. The first was a "palatial-sized" apartment: kitchen, den, bath, and bedroom. The problem was the kitchen sink. It had no drain, so water had to be collected from the sink in a pot and emptied in the bathroom.

The second option was an attic apartment in an old house that had a small kitchen (with drain); a tiny bathroom with a ceiling so low and slanted I had to duck my head to shower; and a bedroom. We took that one and later transferred to married quarters off campus when room became available.

At the time, Dartmouth Medical School only offered the first two years of medical training, so I had to transfer for the last two years. I applied to Harvard Medical School.

The day the acceptance letters were due to arrive, Joan and I stood by the mailbox on the lawn, hearts pounding as the mail truck got closer and closer.

"What do you think?" I asked her. "Yes or no?"

"Of course, yes," she said. "They'd be dumb not to accept you. You're going to be a great doctor." Her faith in me throughout our lives has carried me over lots of tense spots. This was just the first of many to come.

When the mailman arrived, I took the envelope with shaking hands.

"Congratulations. You've been accepted ..."

The joy of that acceptance letter felt like winning the lottery. We were going to Boston! I would learn medicine at the mecca of medical schools.

I recalled some of those memories recently when Dartmouth Medical School invited me back to receive its Distinguished Career Achievement Award. As I accepted the honor, I pointed to Joan, sitting in the second row. "I'm here because of that lady," I said, fighting back tears.

Marty Berman ran Berman Realty, a Boston real estate company his retired father had started. During our first trip to Boston before medical school started, Joan and I lucked out: we found Marty. He rented us an apartment on Park Drive, walking distance from Harvard Medical School; gave Joan a job as his office manager; and became our Medici patron. He called Joan "Honey" and me "Doc." Marty took us to Boston restaurants and shows we couldn't afford, and bought fresh bagels and lox on Saturday mornings before I left for classes.

He visited Indianapolis years later but, after a lifetime living in Boston, said the silence was so deafening it kept him awake all night. During one visit, our son crept into our bedroom early one morning. "The man what's sleeping downstairs, his eyes is open," he said.

When Boston's Beth Israel Hospital was recruiting me to head its cardiology department in the early 1980s, Marty met me at Logan Airport in a chauffeur-driven Rolls Royce, his congratulatory gesture that I had finally arrived. (I declined the job offer at the BI.) We're still good friends more than fifty years later.

17

PARENTS

My father refused to talk to me for three years after our wedding, despite Joan's lack of pregnancy, her working to supplement our income, and my success in medical school. His silent treatment forced me to do one of the most embarrassing things in my life, so demeaning I've never told a soul. Remembering it makes my blood run cold.

Joan and I visited my parents during a school break in my last year at Harvard in 1964, despite my father's silence. Joan was now pregnant with our first child. My mother had appealed to my father—"He's your son, Bob. Enough with the silent treatment"—but to no avail. This was a Zipes family peculiarity: he or one of his brothers could shun another family member for years after an argument.

We were sitting in the tiny kitchen when my mother, trying to spark interaction, said, "I think some rats"—again with the rats—"got into the garbage cans outside. Why don't you help Dad clean it up?"

My father, not speaking, got up and went out the back door. I followed, grim-faced. We worked shoulder to shoulder in total silence, picking up garbage near a wrought-iron fence.

After a while, I couldn't handle it anymore. I saw a wire poking out from the fence, raked the back of my hand on it, and yelled, "A rat just bit me," just to get him to look at me, talk to me, do *something* with me.

He didn't budge.

I went in the house and washed and bandaged the wound. I was mortified that I had stooped so low with my own father. I decided that was the last straw.

When he came back into the house, I said, "This is our last visit. If you don't stop the silent treatment, we're not coming home again. It will be the last time you'll see me, and you'll never see your grandchild." I walked out of the room.

That broke the logjam. Little by little, we rebuilt a relationship. But it would never be the same, at least not from my standpoint. My groveling had left a permanent scar.

My parents moved to Florida when my mother retired from the *Reader's Digest*. Sadly, her retirement ended prematurely when she became ill shortly after the move, and she died from lung cancer a few months later. After her death in 1974, my father turned to Joan and me for emotional support and even discussed moving in with us or getting an apartment nearby. He'd forgiven my apparent transgression.

In 1978, he began having heart rhythm problems following a second heart attack. I suggested he come to Indy for an examination and a trial with amiodarone, a new antiarrhythmic drug I was investigating.

I met him at the airport early one evening and offered him a choice of coming home with me to see the family, and being admitted to the hospital the next morning, or going directly to the hospital from the airport. He chose to come home.

Joan fed him dinner. He played with his three grandchildren and retired early. When I knocked on the guestroom door to wake him the following morning, I got no response. I opened the door.

"Dad," I called, "time to wake up so we can go to the hospital."

No response.

"Dad," I called louder. Still no response.

I went over to him and gently shook his shoulder. It was cold.

He was dead, stretched out on the bed. He'd had cardiac arrest and died in his sleep during the night.

We were all devastated. Had I taken him directly to the hospital from the airport, he would likely have been resuscitated. It was his choice, but I must live with the consequences. He'd never been the same after my mother's death. She was the power source for him, and when she died, a light went out. Perhaps, in his own mind, now darkened, he'd said, "I'm in my son's home. I can relax and just let go."

He's buried next to my mother in the family plot.

PART III

MEDICAL EDUCATION AND TRAINING

18

EUGENE STEAD

I received my medical degree cum laude (with honors) from Harvard Medical School in 1964. From there I went to Durham, North Carolina, for additional training in medicine and cardiology at the Duke University Medical Center.

A major attraction at Duke was the philosophy of Eugene Stead, chairman of medicine, that the patient's interests lay at the heart of all we did and that the best way to learn to take care of patients was to immerse yourself in their care. To accomplish this, Dr. Stead made sure we practically lived with the patient and his illness to absorb all there was to know. As interns, we worked in the hospital six and a half days a week and were on call five nights out of seven. The intern administered the care, chose the diagnostic and treatment strategies with guidance from senior physicians, and learned over the course of the patient's illness whether his choices were correct. It was immensely satisfying and educational.

Joan and I had three children during training, and they often joined me for dinner in the hospital cafeteria. We lived in a tiny duplex house ten minutes from the hospital (ninety-five dollars a month). If the night was calm, I left "early" (midnight) and took hospital call at home. Many nights I would just be crawling into bed, exhausted, when the phone would ring, summoning me back to the hospital for a new admission or because my patient's condition had worsened. After a while, the mere sound of a telephone triggered a Pavlovian response that sent my heart racing and my breathing into overdrive.

Author with children, Debra, David (infant), and Jeff—Durham, North Carolina, 1967.

Dr. Stead arrived on the ward at ten in the morning three days a week. You could almost hear our sphincters snap to attention when he entered the room.

As one of the most important guiding lights in medical education, he presented an unlikely appearance. Lean and lanky, stoop-shouldered with a long face, balding pate, droopy ears, and piercing blue eyes, he could have been the patriarch of a tobacco-farming family. I pictured him leading a pair of mules out to till the soil in rural Durham.

Until he spoke.

Then, all that changed.

His brain functioned on a level different from ours—different from everybody's. He saw things with such clarity, insight, and originality that you said to yourself, *My God, I thought I knew that but not that way.* His words painted concepts in colors and shapes we never imagined, like viewing an event for the first time through a sunlit, multifaceted prism instead of the usual foggy glass pane.

Sometimes we just sat and waited for him to talk. The silence was unnerving, all of us wanting to say something intelligent to end it but fearful that whatever we'd say would sound stupid, or at least would appear stupid to Dr. Stead. During these sessions, he twiddled a pair of long yellow wooden pencils on his desk, their *click-click* the only noise in the room.

He made rounds on each new patient, and we presented their problems to him at the bedside. Back in the interns' room, Dr. Stead dictated his opinion about the patient, starting with, "Just say for me ..." If we had screwed up in caring for the patient, Dr. Stead dictated, "Just say for me this patient needs a doctor." Such an admonishment branded that person for the year.

If we disagreed with Dr. Stead, he'd bet us a nickel he was right. We scoured textbooks and journals to prove our position. Winning that buffalo was the most important thing in our lives, and word quickly spread if we won: "Didja hear? Ol' Steely Blue Eyes lost a nickel this morning."

Dr. Stead made gallop rounds on Sunday mornings, stopping at the bedside of each patient (sometimes thirty or forty in the ward). The intern had to give a two-minute synopsis, without notes, of each patient's illness. Dr. Stead often said he'd rather be making rounds in the hospital on Sunday mornings than be anywhere else.

One morning after a particularly grueling night without sleep, saving a patient in diabetic ketoacidosis, my fellow intern was telling Dr. Stead about a new patient admitted with lung cancer. The discussion focused on whether the cancer had pushed his trachea (breathing tube) to one side. The conversation went on and on, and the intern fell asleep standing near the patient's feet. (We were so sleep deprived, this was not unusual. I'd fall asleep in my soup if dinner lagged.)

As the intern fell across the foot of the bed, he woke and caught himself on his hands, one on each side of the patient's feet. He had the presence of mind to remember the discussion and look lengthwise at the patient's neck to pretend he was eyeing the trachea from a distance, checking for deviation. Dr. Stead, without pause or smile, said, "Well done, son."

The rotation interns looked forward to was a month covering the emergency room. In 1964, Duke's ER was little more than a few rooms, mostly treating students' colds and allergies. It was a month when we could finally catch up on all the hours of lost sleep and even do a little reading. It was a time to replenish our strength—even our sanity—before the final push to the end of the intern year.

Two days after I started in the ER, an undergraduate student presented with a history of a peanut allergy. He had unknowingly eaten a breakfast pastry that contained peanuts buried in the icing. He went back to his room, took an antihistamine, but felt his throat constricting and came to the ER.

Shortly after I began my examination, he gasped once and keeled over, unconscious. I could not record a blood pressure or feel a pulse. I shouted for a nurse to bring me an IV setup and epinephrine to treat anaphylactic shock.

I've inserted thousands of IVs but none as dramatic as this one. Since he had no blood pressure, his veins were flat and could not even be seen. With shaking hands, I shoved a needle into the crook of his arm where I thought the vein should be and—miraculously—hit it on my first try! I injected a bolus of epinephrine, and within a short time, the young man regained consciousness. I gave him a second epinephrine dose, followed by steroids, and his blood pressure returned to normal. I admitted him to the hospital for observation overnight.

I wrote orders in his chart requesting a dietician to instruct him on what foods to avoid and to be certain he received no foods with peanuts.

The next morning—you guessed it—his breakfast tray contained a bun with a peanut topping!

A few days later, the chief resident called me with shattering news that made me want to quit my internship. Another intern had taken ill and I would have to cover his rotation. My month's R and R in the ER had gone up in smoke.

The rotation was neurology. At the time, Duke had no neurology ward, so dozens of neurology patients were scattered all over the hospital, wherever there was an open bed. Since interns had to draw all the blood on their patients before rounds in the morning, I now had to wake up an hour earlier to get to all the patients that needed blood tests. The rest of the day and evening would be spent running all over the hospital caring for these patients, some of whom were acutely ill.

I was crushed, the anticipated ER break snatched from my grasp and replaced by the worst rotation.

Joe LeBauer, from Greensboro, North Carolina, saved me.

Joe was a resident, a year or two further along in training than I, and in charge of neurology that month. He sat me down and, in a calm and patient way, told me he would help with my chores—including blood drawing.

A medical resident doing intern's scut work? Unheard of! But Joe did just that. We shared the workload, and somehow I made it through the month.

I felt so like quitting. The year had been very rough—one intern had already quit—and we all looked forward to the ER sanctuary. If it had never existed, I'm sure I would not have had a problem. But to lose something my heart was set on was especially difficult. I will always be so grateful to Joe for keeping his cool—and mine.

Joe went on to establish a very successful multispecialty health organization in Greensboro.

Dr. Stead and I remained friends after I completed my training, and on occasion I sought his advice. Years later, when I had an interaction with Soviet physicians and questioned whether to maintain a relationship, I called Dr. Stead. I explained that I had disagreed with the Soviet government's invasion of Afghanistan and threatened to quit the NHLBI group to protest the invasion.

I had asked my Russian counterpart to join me. He would have no part of it. His response was "The czar's business is the czar's business; the people's business is the people's business. Why get involved?"

Dr. Stead's reaction was quite precise. "You know, Doug, you can't change how people think—Soviets or anybody else. We've all got brain patterns laid down since we were children, and nothing's going to alter how the brain waves travel over these pathways. My brain never developed to like classical music, so I just don't listen to it. I don't get mad at people who do, and I've never tried to change them or me. That's just the way I was made."

I didn't take his advice and quit the NHLBI group.

Sadly, Dr. Stead stopped teaching in his later years. He told me, "These young doctors are no longer interested in the kinds of questions I ask." His questions often had no clear answers but motivated us to think while trying to find one. This next generation of doctors didn't like that. They wanted concrete questions they could answer by reading a textbook.

HENRY MCINTOSH

19

Shortly after I began my internship, a teenage girl with rheumatic heart disease was admitted to my service. The heart doctors had scheduled her for a catheterization, which involved putting tubes in her blood vessels, threading them back to her heart to measure pressures and to inject dye for x-rays. A routine procedure today usually takes less than an hour. In 1964, it was a major intervention. After three or four hours, she returned to the ward ashen, blood and intravenous medications dripping in to shore up her falling blood pressure. She stabilized after a while, and I assumed she would be headed for surgery the next day.

Not to be. I was told she had to have a repeat heart catheterization the following day because the doctors had not obtained some research data they wanted.

"Is that needed for her surgery?" I asked.

"No," came the reply, "just for research."

"Then you can't do it," I said, exercising my role as the patient's advocate. "Just let her go to surgery."

An hour later, the nurse came into the interns' office. "Dr. McIntosh wants to talk with you."

I had no idea who Dr. McIntosh was. "Fine," I said. "Have him come up."

She gave me a strange look, shrugged, and left.

I wrote a note in the patient's chart that concluded, "There is no

103

clinical need for this patient to be recathed before surgery. This is purely for research, and it places her at additional risk. I will not sign the order to do so in view of her problems yesterday."

Ten minutes later, a dark-haired older doctor, flanked by a junior doctor on each side, burst into the interns' office. I was to learn later that Dr. Henry McIntosh was a leader of men, recipient of a Silver Star, Croix de Guerre, and two Bronze Stars after he parachuted behind enemy lines during World War II. His orders were not to be denied.

"Who's Dr. Zipes?" he demanded, looking around at the startled faces in the room.

I stepped forward, apprehensive. This man exuded confidence and control. I didn't know what I was in for.

"I am."

"Do you know who I am?" he asked.

"No, sir."

"I'm Dr. McIntosh, chief of cardiology."

I gulped. *Oh shit.* Blinded by the responsibility I had felt toward the patient, I had blundered big time.

"What do you mean we can't catheterize your patient? You're the new intern from Harvard, aren't you?"

"Yes, sir."

"You doctors from Harvard think you know better than we do at Duke?" he asked.

"No, sir, it's just that—"

"Let me tell you something, Doctor. Research is important. That's how we advance science and the care of patients. You understand?"

"Yes, sir, I do, but—"

"No buts. You can't stop the catheterization. If you do, she'll be taken off our research grant and must pay for her hospitalization out of her own pocket. Do you understand?"

"Yes, but—"

"Then be sure to change the orders so she can be recathed in the morning." Before I could finish, Dr. McIntosh stomped out of the room.

I was devastated, torn between what I thought was best for the patient and the wishes—demands, really—of the chief of cardiology. Technically, I was the boss of this patient, and nothing could be done without my approval. The reality was different. I was a lowly intern. Even nurses had higher standing.

Once, when an intern and a nurse feuded over some issue or other, Dr. Stead called the intern to his office.

"She's a lot harder to replace than you are, Doctor," he said. "You'd better shape up and get along with her."

If I wanted to stay at Duke, I had to do what Dr. McIntosh wanted. I wrote the order for the repeat cath but added a long note to the chart saying I disagreed with that decision. In retrospect, it was probably the perfect foundation for a malpractice lawsuit today.

I tossed and turned all night and got to the hospital by six the next morning, filled with trepidation. I knew the day would be awful. I only hoped the cath would be quick and less traumatic than the day before.

At a quarter after six, the phone rang in the interns' office. "Dr. Zipes?"

"Yes."

"This is Dr. McIntosh."

My heart flip-flopped, and I broke into a cold sweat. "Yes, sir."

"I've been thinking overnight about your decision, and I decided you're right. We're canceling the cath and sending your patient straight to surgery."

"What about her hospital costs?" I asked.

"The grant will still pay for her hospitalization."

I collapsed into a chair as relief swept over me. "Thank you, sir. I'll get her prepped." I grabbed a Kleenex to wipe my forehead.

"Very good. See that she's ready by seven."

She went to surgery an hour later and did very well.

I had no idea at the time that Henry McIntosh and I would become very good friends, that he would accept my application for a cardiology fellowship at Duke, that we'd coauthor a textbook chapter together, or that he'd try to recruit me to his medical department when he left Duke to become chairman of medicine at Baylor. He eventually became president of the American College of Cardiology. Many years later, when I too became president of the ACC, I instituted an award for international public service and made certain Henry was the first recipient.

But before any of that transpired, he and I would have one more major disagreement.

WALTER KEMPNER

20

Dr. Walter Kempner emigrated from Nazi Germany in 1934 when Duke Hospital recruited him as a medical scientist. Slim, medium height with dark hair, he was a handsome, charismatic autocrat who amassed a group of patients that exceeded in number all other medical doctors at Duke combined.

His attraction? The rice diet.

At a time when no effective therapy existed for diabetes, high blood pressure, or kidney disease, Dr. Kempner had a very ill diabetic patient in the hospital. He wondered whether a bland diet might improve her health by flushing the kidneys to rid the body of toxins; he prescribed a diet of white rice and fruit—and no salt.

After her hospital stay, the patient by mistake continued the same diet as an outpatient since no one had told her to change it. When Dr. Kempner saw her many months later, most of the diabetic vascular changes had reversed, her blood pressure was under control, and her kidney function had improved.

Louis Pasteur noted in 1854 that "chance favors only the prepared mind." Dr. Kempner's mind was prepared. He realized the rice diet had significantly reversed these diseases.

Rice diet therapy was born. Often in medicine, a beneficial treatment preexists understanding how it works. Such was the case with the rice diet.

Patients soon traveled to Duke from all over the United States. They lost weight, their blood pressure dropped, general health improved, and they flocked to Durham in droves. Duke established "rice houses" in town at cooperating motels/hotels to serve rice, fruit, and vitamin supplements to accommodate the overflow from the university hospital.

I was Dr. Kempner's intern for a month's rotation in 1964. Private doctors controlled the care of their private patients, and we interns implemented their orders.

We made rounds in the morning to check on each patient. Dr. Kempner walked stiffly erect, hands clasped behind the back of his starched, long white coat, and stethoscope dangling from earpieces around his neck. He stood for a moment at each patient's bedside and granted them one question, and one question only.

Invariably, they asked about their urine. Dr. Kempner had the hospital collect every drop from every patient and analyze it for salt to see who was cheating. An occasional patient who snuck a pizza slice the day before would offer hard cash to buy the urine of one who had followed the rice rules.

One day a wealthy New Yorker, head of a major corporation, was admitted to Dr. Kempner's service to treat uncontrolled high blood pressure and to lose weight. He was a big guy, more than three hundred pounds, with a huge gut hanging over his belt. Accustomed to giving orders, he struggled with Dr. Kempner's domineering style.

After three weeks in the hospital eating rice every day—except Friday when he was allowed a boiled chicken breast—the patient began to go stir-crazy.

On Thursday, he'd become euphoric, anticipating Friday's chicken dinner. "My God, I can't wait until tomorrow," he'd tell the nurses. "Make sure it comes early."

On Saturday, he plummeted to the depths of depression. "I can't face six more days of rice," he'd complain to whomever would listen.

On the third Saturday, he broke—just lost it. Spotting a tray full of delicious food for the patient across the hall, he bolted from his bed and grabbed the first thing he could—it turned out to be a hard-boiled egg—wolfed it down and, hiding his face with a napkin, snuck back to his bed, hoping no one saw him.

A nurse reported the event to Dr. Kempner.

When we made rounds the next morning, the CEO pinched his brow, squinted his eyes, squirmed, fidgeted in his bed, and looked everywhere but at Dr. Kempner. Dr. Kempner appeared oblivious, aloof, glaring down at him.

Finally, after several silent moments, the patient couldn't stand it any longer and blurted out his one question. "Dr. Kempner, how—um, how—um, how was my urine?"

Dr. Kempner stared him in the eye and without a moment's hesitation said, "Urine? Your urine had one hard-boiled egg in it!" He spun on his heels and stalked out, leaving the patient aghast, his mouth wide open.

The man checked out of the hospital that afternoon and returned to New York on the first flight out of Durham.

One evening, after being on Kempner's service for just a few days, I received an urgent page from a nurse. "The judge is having a seizure. We need you stat."

"The judge?" I asked. "I don't know any judge."

"You are Dr. Kempner's intern, aren't you?"

"Yes."

"He's your patient."

"Was he just admitted?"

I heard her laugh over the phone. "Fifteen years ago."

It turned out the patient was a totally senile, retired judge, admitted to eat rice as a last-ditch effort to save whatever brain function could be salvaged. He occupied a private room, had 24-7 personal nursing care, and received three daily feedings of rice by an implanted stomach tube.

I sedated him, the seizure stopped, and he went to sleep. Each intern prayed the judge didn't die on his rotation because that meant dictating many years of medical history for the discharge summary. After seventeen years in the hospital, the judge expired, and some unlucky intern had major dictation to do.

When we made rice rounds in the morning, an entourage of young doctors, as well as several senior physicians employed by Dr. Kempner, trailed behind. One doctor was an elderly female who performed all the gynecology exams on Dr. Kempner's female patients. We had just started rounds when she turned ashen, became sweaty, and complained of chest pain. She was immediately hospitalized, and an electrocardiogram showed that she had suffered a heart attack. Dr. Kempner asked me to take care of her.

Though the heart attack was mild, that afternoon her blood pressure fell to dangerous levels. She became short of breath and clammy and faded in and out of consciousness. I couldn't figure out what was wrong until I realized she had been eating the rice diet with no salt. She needed saline to raise her blood pressure.

I explained her condition to Dr. Kempner.

"No. Absolutely not. You cannot give salt to my patient" was his response.

Toward early evening, she started to get sicker, but Dr. Kempner was adamant. Lab tests showed she was mildly anemic, and I seized on that fact.

"Can I give her a transfusion?" I asked.

"Blood is okay. No salt," Dr. Kempner said.

I infused a unit of blood and—directly disobeying his order—followed this with one liter of saline. Her blood pressure promptly rose, her clinical course stabilized, and she turned the corner.

I was a hero. That is, until the results of her urinalysis came back.

"Why is there so much salt in her urine, Dr. Zipes?" Dr. Kempner demanded the next morning.

I flushed and fumbled for an answer.

"Maybe she got salty blood, sir," I stammered.

He looked at me a long time, his penetrating, dark eyes boring into my brain, knowing full well this was bullshit. I could see him weighing the situation and deciding what to do. A quick check of the patient's chart would reveal my duplicity. Disobeying an order from the staff doctor was grounds for immediate dismissal from the training program, all my hopes and aspirations dashed.

After an eternity, he nodded briefly, turned, and left. The rest of the gynecologist's course was uneventful, and she returned to work soon after.

Three years later, in my last year of training as a cardiologist, I was writing my first chapter on heart rhythm disorders for a major textbook, with Dr. McIntosh as a coauthor. I desperately wanted to attend a conference on the interpretation of complex electrocardiograms at Michael Reese Hospital in Chicago, but I had no money to pay for such a trip—even though my salary had ballooned to a staggering $300 a month. Duke cardiology claimed poverty, and with regret, Dr. McIntosh said he had no money to send me.

I made an appointment to see Dr. Kempner. Would he remember me? Would he be angry? He could still have me fired for disobeying him.

"Dr. Kempner, do you remember me?" I asked, standing in front of his desk in his office. I wiped moist hands on the sides of my pants.

He set down the medical journal he was reading, pushed back from his desk, and peered at me over glasses perched at the end of his nose.

"Ah, yes," he said, "I do remember. The intern who gives salty blood to my patients." A hint of a smile teased the corners of his eyes, and I relaxed a little. I realized I had been holding my breath, exhaled, and sucked in some air. "What can I do for you?"

I explained I wanted to attend this conference and had no money. "How much do you need?" he asked.

I said, "I think $250 will cover the plane ticket and hotel."

He didn't say a word, opened his desk drawer, and removed a checkbook. He looked up at me for a long second before writing, then down at his checkbook. He penned the check, ripped it from the ledger, and handed it to me. I thanked him and glanced at it—$300.

Before I left, he transfixed me once again with those piercing eyes. "Sometimes it's better to follow your own conscience," he said, pushing his glasses back up the bridge of his nose. He nodded my dismissal and returned to his reading.

REGRETS AND RECOGNITION

Many Hollywood actors regret turning down that one role in a film that went on to become a box office blockbuster and Oscar winner. I lived such an experience at Duke.

During my cardiology fellowship, I took care of a fisherman from the Outer Banks in North Carolina who had an inherited problem called Wolff-Parkinson-White (WPW) syndrome. WPW predisposed him to the development of rapid heartbeats (tachycardia), over two hundred per minute, and required—at the time—herculean efforts to control. The man showed up in my clinic almost weekly with episodes of tachycardia and required a great deal of my time to care for him.

I was very busy writing the chapter on heart rhythm disorders with Dr. McIntosh and didn't have a spare minute. I asked a colleague in the same clinic, Fred Cobb, whether he would mind taking care of this patient. Fred, a wonderful friend and superb cardiologist, agreed.

This patient became the first patient in the entire world cured by a new surgical procedure perfected at Duke by the heart surgeon, Will Sealy, which eliminated the WPW. And Fred, of course, was the first author of the paper that presented this cure to the world. After that discovery, Duke became the mecca for this kind of tachycardia surgery.

Fred specialized in heart failure, so the paper didn't have a major impact on his career, certainly not like it might have had on mine. Sadly, Fred died unexpectedly in 2006 at age sixty-seven.

Some forty years after my experiences with Drs. Stead, McIntosh, and Kempner, Duke awarded me the Distinguished Alumnus Award. In my acceptance speech, I said, "I owe Duke a lot for my education, including $408."

That sparked quizzical looks in the audience, and I went on to explain.

My wife was approaching her due date with our first baby when I graduated from Harvard Medical School and arrived in Durham as an intern in June 1964. An obstetrician, Brian Little, at the Boston Lying-In Hospital had provided free prenatal care at Harvard.

Duke was different. Joan had one visit after we arrived in Durham, delivered the next day, and I was charged $150 for an entire prenatal package. I protested to Dr. Stead, to no avail. Being an intern on staff carried no weight.

I refused to pay that charge when we checked out of the hospital with our new daughter. I was already in debt, borrowing several thousand dollars each year from a medical trust fund just to pay for food and rent. That $150 was huge. Duke tacked on that same initial unpaid $150 after our second and third children were born, and each time I refused payment. When I left Duke, I still owed the original $150.

The second debt occurred because of a bookkeeping error. As an intern, I rotated monthly between Duke Hospital and the Durham Veterans Administration Hospital. Whichever hospital I worked paid me $250 for the month. One month I mistakenly received a paycheck from both hospitals. The temptation to keep both checks was great, but I couldn't. I returned the second paycheck to Dr. Stead's secretary, a wonderful and much-loved woman.

"Doug," Bess said, "the hours required for me to unravel this mess are not worth the effort. Keep the check, and buy Joan a nice dress."

I did, but now I owed Duke $250 for that double payment.

In my last year as a cardiology fellow, I skipped my usual day in the cardiology outpatient clinic one week in late June because I was lecturing at another hospital. Even though I had gotten a replacement, Dr. McIntosh said that was not acceptable. I would be docked one day's pay, worth about eight dollars. A week later, he told me it was too late to deduct it from my final paycheck, already issued, but I had to write a check to Duke Hospital for eight dollars to receive it. I did as ordered and grabbed my last paycheck, and we headed to Portsmouth, Virginia, to start my two years of required service in the US Navy.

Several weeks later, Dr. McIntosh called me and said, "You SOB, your check bounced!" My wife had transferred our bank account to our new bank in Virginia and forgotten to tell me.

I still owe Duke $408, but, as I told the chancellor when he handed me my award, the check's in the mail.

ALFRED PICK AND RICHARD LANGENDORF

Interpreting the squiggly lines on an electrocardiogram is a highly developed skill and was one of the reasons I went into cardiology. The beating heart creates these electrical impulses, but deciphering what they mean and what is happening to the heart can be a challenge.

Once a year, Richard Langendorf and Alfred Pick, two of the world's greatest electrocardiographers, held a weeklong ECG course limited to fifty doctors. Advanced ECG interpretation at Michael Reese Hospital in Chicago was always a sellout. With Kempner's check in hand, I sent off my application and was accepted.

Alfred Pick, date unknown.

Author with Richard Langendorf at a symposium in Dallas, 1985.

I needed a cheap hotel room, so I called the Chicago YMCA. "Sorry, totally booked that week" was the reply. "But wait. You said you're a doctor, right? We have one room left at the YWCA. Being a doctor, you won't be looking at the women, now will you?" I promised him—and my wife—I wouldn't, and that was where I stayed for a week.[1]

It was an interesting week of high-pitched shrieks and laughter, panty-and-bra-clad runs in the hallways, and bouncing ponytails.

Drs. Pick and Langendorf, using the Socratic method of teaching, took turns at the podium. We fifty doctors sat on hard wooden chairs in a room just big enough to accommodate the group. The teachers projected an ECG on a large screen in the front of the room. They handed each doctor in rotation a pair of oversize wooden calipers to measure ECG intervals, and we had to interpret the unknown heart

---

[1] A brief digression: That reminds me of the story of a Jewish boy attending an orthodox synagogue with his father. Women were segregated to the balcony overhead. After a while, the father looked over at his young son and caught him gazing upward at the women's legs. "If you do that again, you'll go blind," he warned the boy. A few minutes passed. The father again looked at his son. The boy was staring upward but this time had covered one eye with his hand.

rhythm. These were not your everyday heart rhythm disturbances. Drs. Pick and Langendorf had selected them from a lifetime of collecting complex tracings. It was a heart-pounding experience to display one's ECG reading skills, or lack of them, in front of one's peers. Each of us silently prayed for an easy arrhythmia to interpret. The calipers trembled in quaking hands, and breathing became suspended. Someone in the audience—sitting at a distance and not under the same pressure—often stage-whispered the diagnosis before the doctor at the screen did, which added to the stress. If the doc at the screen got it right, he returned to his seat victorious, smiling. If not, he wanted to hide under his chair.

Dr. Langendorf was gentle, kindly. Dr. Pick was not. But we learned—oh my goodness, did we learn! By the end of that week, we became champion ECG readers. We returned to our own hospitals as *the* expert. Michael Reese didn't give out T-shirts but could have: *I survived Pick and Langendorf.*

Two years later, I received one of the highest accolades of my career. I had been invited by Dr. Charles Fisch to participate with Drs. Pick and Langendorf in the ECG program at the 1970 American College of Cardiology Scientific Sessions in New Orleans. We each had a turn lecturing to an audience of several hundred cardiologists. My fifteen-minute presentation took me only three months to prepare. I gave my talk—my first major lecture ever—to an enthusiastic audience. Since I was still in the navy, the navy agreed to pay my travel expenses if I lectured wearing my formal navy whites.

After my talk, Fred and Richard came up to me (we were now on a first-name basis) and said, "We feel like we've just had a son." Praise from gods on high. I couldn't wait to get to a phone and tell Joan. Now, almost fifty years later, some senior cardiologists still come up to me and say, "I remember you standing up there as a kid in your white navy uniform."

On a trip to Europe five years later, I sat next to Fred on the plane. He told me a story that has haunted me ever since.

He and Richard were working at different hospitals in Prague, Czechoslovakia, before the Second World War. Richard and his wife, Raya, fled to Chicago in the late 1930s after the Nazis invaded. Fred wasn't fast enough. The Nazis seized him and his wife, Ruth, and sent them to Auschwitz.

"After we exited the boxcar of the train onto the cement platform of Auschwitz," Fred said, "we were separated into two different lines. I could see Ruth but couldn't talk to her. Without thinking, I put my hand in my coat pocket and felt a piece of chocolate the Nazis had missed in their search. I knew Ruth loved candy. Even though guards were all around, holding the leashes on big German shepherd dogs, I bolted from my line to give her the chocolate. The guards clubbed me for disobeying and ordered me to stay in the new line, next to her. All those poor souls in the line I left went to the gas chamber."

After the war, the cardiology division at Michael Reese Hospital was recruiting a doctor to head up their ECG reading service. Richard, busy seeing patients, didn't have the time and suggested they recruit his friend Fred. Not sure of Fred's expertise, the chief of cardiology sent him a very complex electrocardiogram to interpret. Fred offered insight into the heart rhythm problem never before proposed. The hospital recruited him along with Ruth, and they both spent their entire professional careers at Michael Reese.

From the time I took their course until their deaths, Fred and Richard remained my good friends and, of course, demigods.

At their 1968 course, I met a physician from Indiana University Medical Center. He told me that the chief of cardiology at Indiana University was looking for someone with my interests and skills, and he suggested I visit. I did, and there I have remained for the next forty-five-plus years. Had I not given saline to Kempner's patient in 1964, my life's path would have taken a very different course.

US NAVY

I had signed up for the Berry Plan in medical school. The Vietnam War was at its height, and the Berry Plan provided draft deferment to finish medical training before enlisting in the military. Henry McIntosh had a connection with the US Navy and secured a position for me as a staff cardiologist at the US Naval Hospital in Portsmouth, Virginia, one of the navy's largest teaching hospitals.

My two years in the navy (1968–1970) were a great experience: I made $10,000 per year, a huge amount back then; stood watch as officer of the day overseeing the emergency room only twice a month; played golf three times a week—in fact, I won the navy base championship both years—bought our groceries, clothes, and whatevers at a discount in the officers' commissary; and functioned as a teaching and treating cardiologist the entire time. I even published a research paper or two.

I joined the navy reserve as a lieutenant after receiving an hour's instruction on how to be an officer. I knew so little about rank that I crossed to the other side of the street to avoid passing a fellow officer since I didn't know whether I had to salute him, he me, or neither. My ship experience was a three-hour tour of the USS *Forrestal*, dry-docked in Norfolk for repairs after a shipboard fire the year before.

Author and Joan going to formal navy dinner—Portsmouth, Virginia, 1969.

The medical service at the hospital was structured like any teaching hospital, with interns, residents, and cardiology fellows. The chairman of medicine in my first year was Dr. Jack Dempsey, a career navy captain. An affable fellow, Captain Dempsey was strict on protocol. When he and his wife invited us for dinner at his home, the ladies were advised to wear white gloves, and I was expected to leave a calling card in a receiving bowl. Joan had white gloves, but I didn't have a calling card, so I violated protocol in my first week in the navy.

I taught an ECG course once a week patterned after Pick and Langendorf. I projected unknown ECGs on a screen the doctors had to interpret. Captain Dempsey came once. I made the mistake of calling on him to interpret a very difficult ECG, sinus node Wenckebach exit block.

I learned a valuable lesson. Never publically embarrass a superior officer. "Captain Dempsey, would you like to interpret this ECG?" I asked.

He went to the screen, hemmed and hawed, and finally made a stab at the diagnosis. It was wrong, and I showed him the correct interpretation.

"Thanks, Doug. That was a tough arrhythmia," he said.

"Yes, sir, it was. Most people wouldn't be able to interpret it."

He took it well, but the astonished looks on the faces of the cardiology fellows made it clear I had again violated protocol. He never came to my ECG session again.

Joe Horgan replaced Captain Dempsey at the end of the year. Joe (never *Captain* Horgan) was a pipe-smoking golfer, and we hit it off from the start. Joe didn't care much about protocol as long as you did your job. Several years later when Joe made flag rank (admiral), I attended his swearing-in ceremony at Bethesda Naval Hospital.

I performed cardiac catheterizations and staffed the coronary care unit. The navy had an interesting setup that I called reverse prejudice. The ward for enlisted men abutted the CCU, while the officers' quarters were several floors above. After recovery from the acute phase of a heart attack, the patient was moved out of the CCU to convalesce. Enlisted men went to the ward right next to the CCU, while the officers, because of the noise and constant activity of the CCU, were transported to distant quiet rooms. If a patient suddenly developed a life-threatening heart rhythm problem after discharge from the CCU, doctors reached the enlisted man in seconds. The officer could die in the time it took us to race up the stairs to his room.

Many of the cardiology fellows I taught outranked me because they were regular navy and had been promoted multiple times since enlisting in medical school. I made CCU rounds on each patient for two hours in the morning, then left to perform catheterizations or treat outpatients the rest of the day. The cardiology fellow spent his entire rotation caring for patients in the CCU.

During morning rounds one day, I overheard a patient ask the cardiology fellow, who outranked me as a lieutenant commander, "Do you think if Dr. Zipes spent more time on the CCU, he'd learn faster and could then get promoted to lieutenant commander like you?"

I went to the patient's bed. "I'll try harder," I told him.

Earlier I said my only ship experience was on the dry-docked USS *Forrestal*. That's not entirely true. The navy offered sailing lessons, and I signed up. My instructor was a twenty-something little slip of a girl, with skinny arms and legs, tanned from sailing the waters around Norfolk. She took me out in a small sailboat called a dinghy to teach me all I needed to know about sailing in one afternoon.

It was a disaster from the start—or I was. I tripped over ropes, got hit several times by the boom as it swung by, was almost swept overboard twice, and nearly capsized us once. After enduring several hours of my mishaps and mayhem, twenty-something had had enough.

"Dr. Zipes," she said, talking through gritted teeth, "you're the clumsiest person I have ever seen, and there's no way you'll ever learn to sail." She shook her head, sending her blonde ponytail into wicked loops. "You're all thumbs. We're going back to shore before you end up killing one of us."

Dispirited as a sailing flunkout, I got in my car and headed home. Joan was waiting for me with a call from the hospital. A patient had just been admitted with a heart rate of twenty and needed a pacemaker immediately. He was barely conscious and would die soon if we didn't get his rate up.

I raced to the hospital, parked, jumped out of my car, and sprinted to the cath lab. The corpsman had the patient all prepped. The pacing wire I needed to put in his heart was sterilized and waiting for me. I stuck the wire in the patient's vein and threaded it into the right ventricle, the lower chamber of his heart. I steered it as if it had eyes. Fifteen seconds after I arrived in the room, the patient had a steady, paced heart rate of seventy beats per minute and was smiling.

All the while I was thinking what my sailing tutor had said. "Dr. Zipes, you're the clumsiest person I have ever seen."

This patient would have disagreed.

Joan and I were sad to leave the navy and the many friends we had made. The navy tried to get me to re-up but couldn't guarantee an academic position, so I refused. The navy gave me a letter of commendation for my teaching, which was nice. The cardiology fellows gave me a pair of gold-plated ECG calipers mounted in a mahogany base that still sits on my desk after almost fifty years.

24

GORDON MOE

After my two years in the navy, several physicians, including Dr. McIntosh, attempted to recruit me to join their staff. Indiana offered the best opportunity: become an assistant professor of medicine at full salary but study for a year any place I wanted at Indiana's expense.

A sabbatical to start a job? Unheard of. I accepted and chose to work with one of the most brilliant research scientists in the world.

Gordon K. Moe, PhD, MD, directed the Masonic Medical Research Laboratory (MMRL) in Utica, New York.

MMRL was a small, two-storied red brick building that occupied a tiny corner of several well-manicured acres of the Masonic Home for Senior Living in the outskirts of Utica, an old town halfway between Syracuse and Albany. Utica had two jewels: MMRL and Grimaldi's Italian Restaurant. Gordon and a few colleagues had lunch there every day.

"Hiya, Doc," Joe the bartender called out as we walked in. I wanted to shake him and say, "Do you know who you're talking to? This is the greatest electrophysiologist in the world!" But that wasn't Gordon's style. He was Doc to Joe.

Unbidden, Joe prepared Gordon's extra-dry Beefeater gin martini as we sat at the bar. A short, baldheaded, rotund Italian, Joe had been serving Gordon his martini and a bowl of minestrone with crackers for years.

"No olives in the martini," Gordon had once instructed Joe. "If I want a salad, I'll order it. Takes up gin space. Same for ice."

"Joe, give my friend one also," he said, nodding at me. I didn't know what an extra-dry Beefeater gin martini was. I soon found out. Wow!

I accompanied Gordon and friends the first few days, but my liver and wallet couldn't handle the stress, so I bagged my own sandwiches after the first week. Besides, we had mandatory happy hour at five. No matter what I was doing, I had to stop and join the lab group in Gordon's office to sip bourbon and talk shop.

Happy hour was an incredible, exhilarating sixty minutes. Gordon led the discussion. Ideas flew around his office like flocks of birds flitting in and out of tree branches, swooping down to land briefly on Gordon's desk, only to be shooed away by hard facts and replaced by new ideas, new hypotheses. It was the most intellectually exciting time of the day and provided fodder for the next day's or next year's research agenda.

The problem was, at six in the evening, Gordon departed for home while we worker bees had to return to our own labs to finish our experiments. This often took me till nine or ten at night.

Winter evenings were the worst. By that time, my ancient, rusting blue Ford—sitting for hours in the frigid Upstate New York winter—had suffered cardiac arrest and required resuscitation. I had to open the car's hood, unscrew the carburetor cover, suck some gas into it, and coax the Ford back to life. I performed this automotive CPR with numb fingers, holding a shaking flashlight in my chattering teeth. The motor, annoyed at being disturbed, coughed, sputtered, and after several tries, finally displayed a return of spontaneous circulation. Sometimes a colleague working late with me, Carlos Mendez, would turn on the ignition while I warmed up the carburetor.

My winter tires had studs, and despite a total snowfall approaching fifteen feet that winter, I usually made it home in twenty or thirty minutes over snowcapped roads. Only once, after the lab's four-hour, very liquid Christmas party, did I have a problem. A telephone pole seemed to rise out of nowhere to hit the front of my car after I left the parking lot. Six feet of snow packed the base of the pole, so it was like bouncing off a hard marshmallow. I just backed up and maneuvered around it.

Ten minutes later, a snowbank jumped up to snatch my front wheels. This was a bit more serious, because here the marshmallow was soft, and I got stuck in three feet of snow. An hour passed before a snowplow came along and dug me out. Fortunately, plenty of circulating antifreeze protected me from the cold. By the time I arrived home two hours late, Joan had checked with the police and local hospitals to be sure I was still alive.

The year with Gordon was bursting with scientific exploration at its best. We discovered fundamental heart processes and published several important papers. That experience laid the scientific foundation for the rest of my professional career. Gordon was my scientific godfather.

When I started the year, I was very frank with Gordon.

"Gordon, I've had very little basic research experience and don't know whether I'm cut out for it."

"You won't know until you try. Give it a chance," he said. "Anytime you want to quit and return to clinical medicine, just let me know. You're free to go."

I almost took him up on that offer. During my first few months, I investigated how digitalis, a two-hundred-year-old medicine, caused arrhythmias. My experiments yielded confusing results, and I was frustrated and depressed. I had never felt that way caring for patients and wondered whether research was a life for me.

"Joan, I don't think I'm cut out for research."

"Why not?" she asked.

"I'm depressed. None of the experiments are working properly, and I feel like a loser."

As I analyzed the reasons why, I had an epiphany. Patient care yielded positive feedback every day. *Someone* from the group of patients

I treated each day always got better and made me feel good about myself and being a cardiologist.

However, if a lab experiment didn't work, the day was a complete bust, with no positive feedback, and I felt like a failure. Once I understood why I was depressed, the laboratory disappointments became tolerable, and I realized that my professional career would always require my having one foot in the laboratory but the other at the bedside caring for patients.

And that was how I spent the next forty-plus years.

Several years after training with Gordon, I had an opportunity to repay him for his many kindnesses. The American College of Cardiology invited me to introduce him to receive an honorary fellowship. In a heartfelt tribute, I planned to tell the packed audience about this generous, loving man who, in addition to his scientific genius, cultivated roses, built furniture (losing a couple of fingertips in the process), enjoyed practical jokes (he left his replacement at Syracuse a giant horse condom to which he had pinned the note, "Dear Jim: I know you can fill my shoes, but ..."), and befriended every person in the lab.

Once, we had invited Gordon to deliver a keynote lecture to a sophisticated arrhythmia group, the Cardiac Electrophysiology Society. He gladly accepted but warned he was battling a sore throat and would appreciate having a large pitcher of water on the table to keep his throat moist. Unbeknownst to Gordon, a dear colleague, Mike Rosen, had the hotel maître d' fill the water pitcher at the podium with Beefeater's gin. Gordon, throat dry, took his first sip, wrinkled his brow, sniffed the glass, and smiled.

"Good water," he said and went on lecturing. His lecture got even better and the jokes funnier as he drained the pitcher. He finished to a standing ovation, put his arm across my shoulder, and said, "I need a drink. Let's go to the cocktail reception."

At the ACC, I sat on the dais next to Gordon waiting for his turn to receive the award. My heart began to pound, and my stomach churned when I heard the precise litanies of the other presenters. They detailed their awardees' accomplishments, including the number of publications they had written, honors, lectures given, and so forth. I had penned nothing of the kind but had this passionate recounting of Gordon's human side, the many trainees he had touched around the world, all of whom loved this giant and took him to dinner whenever he visited their country.

Gordon Moe (hand on face) and author on the dais to receive an Honorary Fellowship Award of the American College of Cardiology, 1976.

Author, ACC presentation for Gordon Moe, 1976.

Distressed, I reached through my ceremonial robe and extracted my presentation. I took out a pen and desperately tried to remember facts about Gordon's academic career. I glanced into the audience where Joan sat in the front row. Our eyes locked, and she shook her head no, just a tiny twitch no one else saw. Across the open space, husband and wife had communicated telepathically. She knew what I was about to do and told me not to do it. I returned the pen to my pocket, gave my original presentation, and Gordon was thrilled with it.

CHARLES FISCH

25

From Utica, we moved to Indianapolis, where I began my career at IU. I promised Joan we'd stay there just a few years as payback for my sabbatical and then be on our way to Southern California. Almost fifty years later, we're still in Indy, now surrounded by our children and grandchildren.

Charles Fisch, chief of cardiology at Indiana University Medical Center and the Krannert Institute of Cardiology, recruited me to Indianapolis in 1970. He was a prominent clinical cardiologist who would later become president of the American College of Cardiology.

When I met Gordon Moe in Utica, he shook my hand and said, "Call me Gordon." Not so with Dr. Fisch. He was always Dr. Fisch, except to his very first trainee, Harvey Feigenbaum (who, after a year, abandoned Dr. Fisch's tutelage to initiate his own groundbreaking research in echocardiography). Harvey was one of the few at the medical center who addressed Dr. Fisch as Charlie.

Dr. Fisch founded the Krannert Institute of Cardiology at Indiana University School of Medicine in 1963 with support from his patient, Herman Krannert, and was intent on building a first-class cardiology program. Herman and his wife, Ellnora, were millionaire philanthropists who supported many educational and cultural projects throughout the Midwest. The Krannerts had made their money from Inland Container, a company that manufactured corrugated fiber products. With no children, they were focused on distributing their wealth for outstanding causes.

I met the Krannerts during my first week at IU in 1971, after I finished my sabbatical with Gordon Moe (which their money had supported). They were seated in Dr. Fisch's Krannert office chatting when I entered. Herman Krannert, then in his eighties, rose from his chair with great effort to shake my hand standing up. He was physically frail but mentally sharp.

"Ah, yes, Dr. Zipes," he said, "it's good to finally meet you. How was your time spent with Dr. Moe? Productive, I hope."

"Thank you, sir," I said. "I appreciated the opportunity to study with Dr. Moe. It was a great year. I learned a lot, and we made some important discoveries."

About a year later, while vacationing in Clearwater, Florida, Herman Krannert had a syncopal episode. He had been preparing for a bath and tumbled into the tub, hitting the hot water faucet as he fell. He suffered third-degree burns over most of his body and was not doing well at the local hospital.

Dr. Fisch called me into his office late one afternoon. "I'm flying to Clearwater in the Krannert jet to bring Mr. Krannert back to IU so we can take care of him at the University Hospital. I want you to come with me."

After outfitting the plane with emergency equipment, we flew to Florida that evening. I examined Mr. Krannert in the hospital. He was unconscious, and his blood pressure was unstable, supported by multiple IV medications. I concluded he was too ill to move and didn't think he'd survive the trip. Dr. Fisch was reluctant to leave him but agreed with me. Herman Krannert died later that night. His wife died of a stroke several years later.

Early on, life at Krannert was terrific. Dr. Fisch and his confidant, Suzanne Knoebel, a beautiful woman, one of the first female cardiologists in the United States, and the first female president of the American College of Cardiology, could not have been more supportive, more generous. They even lent me the down payment on the house I bought and waived the interest. Dr. Fisch made certain I had a nice office at Krannert—he let me pick out my rug, desk, and chairs. He supplied me with my own secretary, a technician for my basic research, and all the equipment necessary to perform experiments. He protected my time from outside distractions so I could focus on research. Saturdays, after a morning of work at Krannert, he, Suzy, Paul McHenry (an early Krannert physician), and I would go for lunch. Dr. Fisch always paid. He and his wife, June, regularly hosted dinners at their home for Krannert staff and heart doctors in training.

Once I joined Krannert, I began to attend the major heart meetings regularly to present my research. One trip to the American Heart Association Scientific Sessions early in my career was memorable.

The meeting was held in Miami. I booked a late-arrival reservation at the Fontainebleau Hotel. When I arrived at about one in the morning, the desk clerk informed me he had given my room to another traveler.

He was a short, skinny guy with pockmarked cheeks and a crew cut, probably a recent hire stuck with the late-night shift.

"How can that be?" I asked, waving the confirmation letter. "I had a guaranteed paid reservation."

The clerk shrugged. "I'm sorry, sir. We're totally full. Many doctors booked rooms."

Another traveler standing alongside me at the desk identified himself as a cardiologist also attending the AHA meeting. "They did the same thing to me. Guaranteed reservation and no room," he said.

I turned back to the clerk. "It's now," I checked my watch, "one thirty in the morning. There's no way I'm leaving to search Collins

Avenue for another hotel room tonight. I intend to sleep in this hotel, even if it's on one of your pretty couches in the lobby." I nodded at the plush foyer behind me, took off my jacket, and loosened my tie. "So, if you don't want me undressing and going to sleep right here, you'd better find me a room."

His eyes got big at my threat. "Please excuse me a moment," the clerk said, "and let me check on something."

He disappeared into a room behind the check-in desk and reappeared moments later. "I have one room left—it's a suite. Would the two of you mind sharing it? Only for tonight. We'll transfer you to a private room in the morning." I suspect his supervisor gave him permission to use the suite rather than me sleeping in the lobby.

I locked eyes with the man standing next to me. We both nodded and shook hands. "I'm Jim," he said.

"I'm Doug."

Problem solved—or so I thought.

The clerk gave us each a key, and I boarded the elevator, got off on the sixth floor, and walked to the suite. I arrived before Jim did. The suite had a small bedroom with two single beds separated by a little night table. The adjacent living room had a sofa that converted to a bed. I decided I'd be the good guy and take the sofa bed. That way we'd sleep in separate rooms.

I removed the cushions and pulled a bar that released the bed folded and stored beneath the sofa. As it sprang open, dust flew everywhere. The blanket and sheet were filthy, the pillow nonexistent. The bed had clearly not been used in some time, and no one had bothered to clean and refresh it since its last use. I decided we'd each take one of the single beds in the bedroom. Though a bit awkward sleeping in the same room with a strange guy, we did have separate beds, and it was better than the alternative. I hoped Jim didn't snore.

I began to undress when the doorbell rang. I figured it was my new roommate. I opened the door.

Hi," Jim said. "I'd like to introduce you to my wife, Sally."

I gulped and stood there speechless. After a moment, I recovered and shook hands with Sally. "Why didn't you say something when we checked in?" I asked Jim.

"I didn't want to blow the chance for a room," Jim said. "There's no way the clerk would've let Sally and me share the suite with you."

I held open the door, and they walked in.

Then I explained the situation. "The sofa bed is not usable. Too dirty. So, unless you have another idea, we'll have to sleep in the single beds."

Jim looked at Sally. She nodded.

"Also, there's only one bathroom. We'll have to share that," I said.

Sally and Jim went first. They got undressed in the bathroom while I did the same in the bedroom. I turned away as they slipped into bed. When I went to the bathroom, Sally held the sheet over her head as I walked by their bed. "Not looking," she said, giggling.

I don't remember much about the night. I guess we all slept soundly. No one snored.

The morning's toiletries were similarly divided for privacy. They dressed in the bathroom, and I dressed in the bedroom. We parted, none the worse for wear.

Later in the day, I happened to see Sally standing with a group of women at the meeting. I shouted a hello; she smiled and waved. Then in a loud voice I said, "I enjoyed sleeping with you last night." She burst out laughing.

I'm sure she had some explaining to do to her friends.

I have given many invited lectures all over the world during my career but none as unique as the one I gave during the early years after joining Krannert. I had been invited to lecture aboard a cruise ship leaving Fort Lauderdale with a group of physicians and nurses and sailing the Caribbean for a week. It would be Joan's and my first cruise—all expenses paid in return for a few lectures. What a blast.

But I had a major problem. I had already committed to lecture in

Philadelphia the morning the cruise departed Fort Lauderdale. Joan was disappointed when I told her I couldn't accept the invitation.

I called the organizer and explained my dilemma. He was as disappointed as Joan and said he'd get back to me.

A week later, he called to let me know he had worked it all out. He told me to give my lecture in Philly, board the first flight to Fort Lauderdale, and he'd take care of the rest.

So, Joan flew to Fort Lauderdale with our luggage the day before sailing and boarded the cruise ship dockside the next morning.

On the same day Joan left for Fort Lauderdale, I flew to Philly. I gave my lecture at eight o'clock the following morning. As soon as I finished, I rushed to the airport and grabbed the first flight to Fort Lauderdale, about two and a half hours long. When I landed, a man met me at the airport, whisked me to a waiting car, and we tore through traffic to the Fort Lauderdale pier. When we arrived, we could see the cruise ship far in the distance traveling out of the harbor to the open ocean.

The driver pulled up on the dock next to a sleek, red speedboat with motor idling. In it was a reporter and photographer from the Fort Lauderdale newspaper. I jumped in, and we left with full throttle roaring, wake churning, chasing the huge cruise ship. A small crowd on the pier clapped and shouted, "Go, go, go!"

My wife later told me she was standing on the top deck watching us approach in the far distance when suddenly the big ship slowed. A woman standing beside her turned and said, "Oh my goodness. Do you think there's something wrong with the motor so early in the cruise?"

Joan played innocent and said, "Gosh, I have no idea."

With the cruise ship barely moving, we began to close the gap and, after ten minutes at a bouncing, breakneck pace, the speedboat pulled alongside. Crewmen dropped a rope ladder over the side of the cruise ship.

I climbed onto the prow of the speedboat as it steadied near the big ship. The water was calm, and the cruise ship was almost stationary. When we were a foot apart, I leaped to the rope ladder as the photographer snapped away and the reporter jotted notes in a notebook.

My foot hit a rung, and I grabbed the rope ladder with both hands. I climbed fifteen or twenty feet until I reached the crew. It seemed like ten hands grabbed at me—my shirt, my pants, my arms and legs. They dragged me into the ship, and I was on board! Then they threw a rope to the speedboat. Someone tied the end to my briefcase, and a crewman hauled it up.

Author climbing up the cruise ship rope ladder, around 1975.

The cruise ship blasted its horn in one long screeching bellow, and we headed into the Atlantic.

The next day the Fort Lauderdale newspaper splashed a picture of me on the front page in suit jacket and tie, clinging to the rope ladder, smiling and waving. Headlines said, "Zipes Zips Up the Ladder. Doctor Delivered at Sea!"

During lunch one Saturday after I had been at Krannert for about six months, Dr. Fisch shared with me a personal philosophy. "Academia is like swimming, Doug. If your head dips too low and you go under, we're here to pull you up. But if your head gets too high, we're here to push it down."

That was exactly what happened. When I became more prominent—especially after Eugene Braunwald, one of the world's leading cardiologists, tried to recruit me in the early 1980s to head cardiology at the Beth Israel Hospital in Boston and I almost left IU for Harvard—Dr. Fisch's and Suzy's support began to wane.

It was the early days of computers, and I requested one to keep track of patient data. Overnight, Dr. Fisch formed a Krannert Computer Committee, chaired by Suzy, that had to approve all computer requests. "No, you can't buy one," she said for no particular reason. I knew that had to have come from Dr. Fisch. Several years passed before she granted her approval.

When I needed an illustration made for a publication or for a lecture, I brought the original ECGs or figures to Dr. Fisch's office. His secretary sent them to the illustrator, and I returned a week or so later to pick them up. Krannert paid the expenses.

One day when I went to his office to get my illustrations, his secretary said, "No, that's Dr. Fisch's pile."

I looked through the slides and glossy prints and said, "You're mistaken. These are mine."

"No, these are yours," she said, pointing to a different set.

"Then what are these?" I asked, nodding at the first pile.

"Those belong to Dr. Fisch. He makes a copy for himself of everything you send."

Dr. Fisch published a textbook in 1990 on clinical electrocardiography of arrhythmias. It included a selection of my ECG illustrations—without attribution to me. I was furious, but he was the chief, and there wasn't much I could do about it. I didn't even bother confronting him. We'd only get into an argument I couldn't win.

In the 1980s, our income at Krannert was based on what we personally billed and collected for our services. When the subspecialty of cardiac electrophysiology (EP) became clinically recognized and in demand, the number of patients our EP group cared for and the number of procedures we performed increased dramatically, as did our collections. However, all money funneled through Dr. Fisch to be distributed to us.

Dr. Fisch decided that, since our collections were so robust, he and Suzy were entitled to 10 percent. Because Dr. Fisch had been so generous and helpful to me at the beginning of my career, providing everything necessary for me to succeed, including the sabbatical with Gordon Moe, I accepted the tithe with only minor grumblings under my breath.

We interacted as colleagues, and on the surface and to outsiders, all seemed to be going well. However, as I was gaining national and international stature, his support continued to wane.

As an example, in 1992, I was chairman of the American College of Cardiology's Young Investigators' Award Committee. After I made my annual status report to the ACC Board of Trustees one year, Jeremy Swan, a friend and chief of cardiology at Cedars Sinai Hospital in Los Angeles, asked, "Why aren't you on the board?" I just shrugged, keeping

Dr. Fisch's swimming philosophy private. Jeremy said, "I'll remedy that." Shortly thereafter, he nominated me to join the board of trustees.

Later, two other non-IU colleagues, Tony DeMaria at UCSD and Rich Popp at Stanford, nominated me for ACC vice president, leading to my presidency in 2001.

Dr. Fisch retired as director of Krannert and chief of cardiology in 1990. The chairman of medicine, after conferring with Dr. Fisch and Suzy, passed over me and selected a basic scientist at Krannert as the new director and chief of cardiology.

My first reaction was denial, thinking it must have been a mistake. As a prominent cardiologist, I thought I'd be the natural choice. When the decision sank in, I became angry. I could understand Dr. Fisch's motivation to not want me as his successor, but the chairman of medicine was my friend. He and I had started at Krannert together as assistant professors. I felt that he and Dr. Fisch had betrayed me, and I was devastated.

Joan and I had scheduled a wonderful lecture-vacation trip to Indonesia and Malaysia, including a stay on the island of Bali, but I couldn't enjoy it, even with our own private villa and swimming pool. She spent much of the vacation consoling me, trying to drag me out of my depression.

Author at the Snake Temple, Penang, Malaysia.

Working through Kubler-Ross's stages of grief, I accepted the change as my anger ebbed, and I attempted to work with the new head of cardiology. The sad thing was, at a time when competing cardiology groups in Indianapolis were gobbling up patients and territory, the new chief wanted Krannert to do nothing of the kind. After all, we were Krannert physicians. Patients would always prefer coming to us. Had I been chief, we would have been in that market, head-to-head with our competition.

After almost four years of mismanagement, the basic scientist was sacked. IU had a new chairman of medicine, Craig Brater, who selected me as director of Krannert and chief of cardiology. By then, Krannert had lost five golden years of potential community outreach and growth.

As the new chief, I made certain that Dr. Fisch and Suzy each had an office and secretarial support, even though their health began to deteriorate and they were no longer contributing meaningfully to our efforts. Upon his death in 2002, Dr. Fisch left a rich legacy of research. When Suzy died in 2014, she supported that effort with a generous bequest of nearly $8.5 million to the Charles Fisch Cardiovascular Research Endowment. It now supports research at the Krannert Institute of Cardiology.

In 2010, the Indiana University president, Michael McRobbie, presented me with the university's highest award, the President's Medal, one of the highlights of my professional career.

PART IV

PATIENTS AND LITIGATION

26

HOUSE CALL TO SAUDI ARABIA

I took an infrequent vacation in 2006. Joan and I were enjoying our first safari and had returned to base camp after an outing on the Serengeti Plain (I wrote about this trip in a short story, "Into Africa," published in two parts by the *Saturday Evening Post* March/April and May/June 2006). I logged onto the camp's computer to catch up on emails. That act triggered what would be one of the most stressful days of my life—perhaps not quite like the KGB experience, which presented physical as well as emotional risk, but close.

Author on safari, Serengeti Plain, 2006.

I read through the usual correspondence, leaving one from a doctor in Saudi Arabia for last. He inquired whether I would make a house call to the kingdom to evaluate a young girl and her mother. Both complained of palpitations. He offered first-class airfare and a "name your fee" stipend.

Fifteen years earlier, just before Desert Storm in 1991, I had cared for two very important Saudi women who had traveled to Indianapolis with a daunting entourage of about thirty or forty people, including relatives, doctors, bodyguards, nurses, and attendants. They had wanted to make their visit inconspicuous, but parking a Boeing 747 labeled in bold letters "Saudi Arabia" on the modest Indianapolis airport tarmac for two weeks was hardly a way to keep a secret.

The group commandeered several rooms of the CCU for their entire stay, with armed guards sitting at the doors. At the end of their visit, one of the women, ready to be discharged, sat on her bed having her hair combed and braided by an assistant. As I was giving her final discharge instructions, she asked, "Dr. Zipes, do you have any children?"

"Yes," I said, "three."

"Boys or girls?"

"Two boys and a girl."

The assistant handed her a leather pouch with a drawstring. The patient reached into her purse and drew out two large handfuls of gold coins and deposited them into the leather pouch. "These are for the boys," she said.

She reached into her purse again, this time with her thumb and forefinger, and withdrew a couple more coins. "For the girl," she said, smiling and handing me the leather pouch. Regretfully, because we needed the money, I sold them to a jeweler for the price of the gold. I wish I had kept at least *one*.

The evening before the Saudis left, the woman's son held a thank-you dinner in my honor. He bought out the restaurant in the hotel in which they were all staying. I warned my wife about Saudi customs. "No drinking, no smoking, and no off-color discussions about sex."

After we were all seated, our host snapped his fingers. "Waiter, champagne for our guests." He then opened a pack of cigarettes and began a discussion about the multiple women in his life.

Back at the safari camp, I emailed the Saudi doctor that I was unavailable at present but could travel in several months. The family found that acceptable, and I made flight arrangements after I returned to the States.

When it came time for my trip, I was accorded VIP status at every turn. First-class travel on Saudi Arabian Airlines was a heavenly trip. The very private first-class compartment rivaled a stay in any luxury hotel— caviar and fine wine, foie gras and rack of lamb divinely prepared, silk pajamas to sleep, and a fully reclining bed with snowy white linens. I woke refreshed, had eggs Benedict for breakfast, and we were there.

A livery-clad driver met me at the airport and drove me to a five-star hotel in the center of the city. After a brief rest, a private guide took me sightseeing for several hours in the afternoon. My physician colleague met me for dinner at the hotel (no wine here), and I retired early.

The following morning, the physician met me in the hotel lobby and drove me to the clinic for my consultation. In an outpatient setting, I evaluated the mother and her sixteen-year-old daughter with a careful history and physical examination. An electrocardiogram showed that the mother had simple premature beats and only required reassurance. I suggested she give up smoking her hookah, but she greeted that with a laugh and a negative headshake.

The daughter described paroxysmal episodes of a rapid heartbeat, around two hundred per minute, that left her dizzy and frightened. Review of an electrocardiogram recorded during an episode made the diagnosis obvious. She had atrioventricular nodal reentry, a rapid heart rhythm easily cured during a heart catheterization procedure. I explained all this to the doctor, mother, and daughter. Though several electrophysiologists in Europe were performing the procedure, my Saudi patients insisted on having it done in Indianapolis. We picked a date several months hence, and they made plans to fly daughter, mother, brother, doctor, nurse, and bodyguard by private jet to Indy. With a defiant smile, the mother assured me she would bring her own hookah on the plane.

27

THE TRIAL

Around the same time, I was preparing to testify as a plaintiff's expert witness against a major drug company.

I have served as an expert witness for many years and have enjoyed the challenge of working in a discipline outside medicine. While I have been an expert witness for both defense and plaintiff litigation, and decide whether to take a case based solely on its merits, most law firms don't cross the divide. They stick to either defense or plaintiff cases.

Defending a claim versus initiating one appeals to different personalities. Defense lawyers generally are not risk-takers, not gamblers. Plaintiff lawyers happily roll the dice.

The two groups remind me of animals I observed on the Serengeti. Defense lawyers are the wildebeests of litigation: large numbers, content to eat an assured daily supply of grass. Plaintiff lawyers are the lions: much fewer in number, often going days without eating, but once they make a kill, they gorge.

The present case involved allegations that the drug company had concealed cardiovascular side effects of its new anti-inflammatory drug and that the drug had injured vulnerable people by causing heart attacks and strokes.

The lawyer for whom I was testifying (I'll call him Bill—he's too well known to give his real name) asked me to come ten days before I was to testify, to prepare for the trial and to provide advice as the trial unfolded. Since the date was around the time the Saudi patient was coming to Indianapolis, I reminded Bill several times to be sure to schedule my testimony so I had time to get home and be with the Saudi family. He assured me he would put me on the witness stand in plenty of time to do that.

Bill was a superb litigator, listed each year as one of the top lawyers in the country. He had a flypaper memory, impeccable shoot-from-the-hip decision-making, and show-stopping ability to multitask. It was rare to be the only person talking to Bill at any one moment. Usually he had a phone to his ear, an associate in front of him, and me alongside, all competing for his attention. He exuded charm that spun friendships with other lawyers and judges, the rugged good looks and physique of a past athlete, and a handsome smile that juries loved.

I was testifying as an expert clinical cardiologist, focusing on the clinical impact of the drug. I was to discuss a patient who had had a heart attack after taking the drug, whom Bill had sent to me for evaluation. An epidemiologist would testify about the many clinical studies the drug company had performed to evaluate the drug, and a science expert would testify on how the drug produced its chemical effects.

The doctor to testify on the chemical action of the drug came to the lawyers' war room at the hotel where we all were staying to practice his testimony. (Each law firm had rented an entire hotel floor.) When the lawyers primed him for trial by subjecting him to a mock cross-examination, asking questions and using techniques the defense attorneys were likely to employ, the scientist balked. "That's what it'll be like on the witness stand? No way I'm going to sit through that. I'm outta here." He left within the hour.

Bill, unfazed, said, "No problem. Doug can give his testimony."

The physician to testify on the outcomes of this drug's myriad clinical trials was elderly and had recently been hospitalized for heart failure. He was so weak Bill had flown him from Los Angeles by private jet. The plane trip, even by private jet, had wiped him out. He became exhausted during the practice cross-examination and had to lie down to rest.

"I can't do it," he said. "So sorry, but there's no way I'd last several hours on the witness stand."

Again, Bill decreed, "No problem. Doug'll handle his part."

I was now the designated expert clinician, scientist, and epidemiologist. I had to testify in two areas for which I was not totally prepared. I spent the remaining days and nights boning up on the additional material I had to know. My testimony would likely span a full day on the witness stand.

I called Joan each evening and vented my increasing anxiety over the delay in giving my testimony and the additional work Bill kept piling on. "I'm reaching my limits," I said.

"Tell him no, you can't," she said.

"He's got no one else," I said. "Somebody has to do it."

Despite my repeated requests to testify, Bill finally gave me the nod only a day before the Saudi family was to arrive in Indianapolis. I would have to fly home right after my testimony. The heart procedure was scheduled the following morning.

Because I was a bit unsure of all the facts attached to my two new hats, I carried to the witness stand a handful of notes about the areas I had recently inherited.

"Your Honor," the defense lawyer was quick to ask the court before we started, "may we please have a copy of Dr. Zipes's notes?"

I looked at him and blinked in surprise. No one had told me the opposing side was entitled to see information I brought to the witness stand. My notes contained all the points I had to cover, as well as potential responses to queries defense might ask. Surrendering them was like telling the Nazis that Allied forces planned to invade Normandy on June 6, 1944. I was devastated and vulnerable, but there was nothing I could do. The opponents now had my game plan.

Painfully, I handed my notes to the court bailiff. He had to jerk them from my fingers and did so with a sympathetic look. His shrug seemed to say, "Not my decision." The bailiff passed the notes to the defense lawyer. He handed them to a paralegal who scurried off to make copies.

As I was sworn in, my eyes wandered the courtroom. I took in the two long, rectangular, wooden tables on opposite sides of the room. They were mirror images, one for plaintiff and the other for defense teams. The judge sat behind an impressive desk, the tallest structure in the courtroom, his back to the wall, flanked by Old Glory and state flags. The witness stand was alongside. The bailiff stood leaning against the wall to one side, and the stenographer sat immediately below the judge's desk.

I was convinced I was the most anxious person in the courtroom. For the judge, the courtroom was his kingdom. "Sustained" or "overruled" was his law, laid down without too much discussion or dissention. Seasoned lawyers knew not to argue too much with his decisions. True, the judge had to get it right, or his decision might be grounds for an appeal, but it seemed easier than my job.

The lawyers had carefully planned what questions they were going to ask. While they didn't always know the exact answers they would get, if they practiced the truism they learned in law school—never ask a question without knowing the likely answer—they wouldn't be too surprised.

For the witness—me—it was like being on stage as the lead actor in a play without a script, a high-stakes drama with the last act still unwritten. Bill had prepped me about questions he would ask, but the other lawyer was an unknown. The setting was not my comfortable lab or office, where I was in total control. Or even a lecture hall where I could ask for my first slide at the start of a lecture.

Opera buffs claim that operatic tenor Luciano Pavarotti paced up and down fighting stage fright before the curtain rose on an opera. "Why in God's name am I doing this?" he would rant. Once the opera started, his nervousness melted away. I felt the same way and hoped mine would as well.

28

TESTIMONY

The trial went something like this:

Bill opened with the direct examination, and I spent the morning answering softball questions we had prepared at length. I hit home run after home run. My nervousness dissipated, and I began to relax, just like Pavarotti.

Big mistake.

After the lunch break, the defense lawyer took over. I'll call him Sam. He accelerated the trial to a different level, throwing hundred-mile fastballs and sliders right at me.

Sam was a tough litigator who prided himself on never having lost a defense case. He was trim with sharp features, dressed in a blue suit, white shirt, and checkered-blue tie. I'd been barred from the courtroom until my testimony, but Bill told me that Sam's opening statement to the jury at the start of the trial, several days before, included a picture of me with the description "paid litigator," implying my testimony might have been bought.

Sam was in my face constantly, both figuratively and literally. He would ask the judge "permission to approach the witness," and thrust his face within inches of mine during my interrogation.

We had a midafternoon break, after which Sam seemed to slow down. He took more time with the questions, pored over his notes, and even seemed to walk more slowly. Something was up; I could feel it.

The fast balls were gone, replaced by unhurried questions, still hard to answer but time-consuming.

Finally, at five thirty Sam stopped and said to the court, "Your Honor, this is a good time to stop. We can resume Dr. Zipes's testimony tomorrow morning."

He watched my face fall and said, "Oh, Dr. Zipes, didn't you know we would have you back? We'll see you again tomorrow morning bright and early."

I was stunned, and my body language showed it. Somehow, Sam must have found out I had to leave town and was taking full advantage of it.

The judge excused the jury. I could barely contain my fury until they left. Standing in front of the judge's bench, I managed an even tone, though I was raging inside, "Bill, I told you I had a patient flying in today from Saudi Arabia and that I had to get home tonight. I'm not staying tomorrow. My promise to my patient trumps my testifying."

Bill turned to the judge. His face was red, but he maintained his cool. "Your Honor, can we have a day's continuance? My expert has to be home tomorrow for professional business."

The judge considered Bill's request. "It's fine with the court if defense agrees." He turned to Sam. "Counselor?"

"No, absolutely not," said Sam, stomping back and forth in front of the judge's bench. His face was contorted into dark lines with a scrunched brow and set lips. I couldn't tell if it was an act or whether he was that angry. "We will not agree to any delays. I have my own witnesses lined up, and this will destroy the timing of my defense. No way, Your Honor." If it was an act, he missed his real vocation.

The judge fiddled with some papers on his desk before answering. "Bill," he said, looking at my lawyer. "Your poor timing leaves me two options, neither pleasant." Bill's face blanched. "I can call a mistrial, and we start over. Nobody wants that. Or I can throw out Dr. Zipes's entire testimony, tell the jury to ignore everything he has said, and we can proceed without him. Your call. What do you want me to do?"

Sam stopped pacing and stood, a smug look on his face. From the witness list, he knew I was now the expert for three lines of evidence and my testimony was crucial to the case. If it were scrapped, he'd win hands down.

"You won't stay?" Bill asked, a pleading look on his face.

I shook my head. "I told you ten days ago I had to get home by tomorrow. The promise to my patient comes first."

I could see the wheels spinning in Bill's head as he calculated risks and benefits. Though Bill was a superb lawyer, one of the very best, he had misjudged his opponent's spy network. Somehow, I think Sam had learned I had to get home, and he had stretched testimony to the next day.

Bill turned to Sam with a resigned expression, shoulders sagging. "I have my final two witnesses scheduled after Dr. Zipes. I'm willing to dismiss them and conclude with Dr. Zipes's testimony if you will agree to a day's continuance."

Sam tried to hide a smile. These were key witnesses, knowledgeable about this drug company and the governmental approval process of this drug. He recognized a bargain when he heard one. He nodded. "Done."

"Then we all have a break tomorrow, an unexpected day off," the judge said. He turned to me and nodded. "Dr. Zipes, we'll see you the day after tomorrow. Remember—you're still under oath and are not to discuss the case with anyone other than your lawyer." He rose from the bench and left.

We exited the courtroom, and I could barely suppress my anger. When we were alone, I exploded. "Goddamn it, Bill. You *knew* I had to leave. Why didn't you put me on earlier?"

He shrugged. There was nothing to say. "I'm sorry. I thought you'd be done in a day. I had no idea Sam would take so long."

He put a friendly arm around my waist, trying to quiet me with his well-known charm. "I'll get you a plane to Indy tonight, you do your patient thing tomorrow, and the same plane will fly you back when you're done with your patient. How's that?"

I was silent, fuming. I had no choice.

Bill called his assistant, told her to get me a jet right away, and we went back to his office. I was so angry I didn't want to be in the same room with him.

"You didn't tell me I had to give them my notes," I said, steaming mad.

"I didn't know you were going to bring them to the witness stand," Bill countered.

"I wouldn't have if I was just giving my original testimony. You tacked on some other stuff, remember?" I flattened my lips, biting back expletives bursting to erupt. "Now they have my complete strategy and the next twenty-four hours to plan their attack using my notes." I shuddered, thinking about Sam's cross-examination when I got back. It promised to be brutal.

Bill backhanded my comment, sweeping it away. "Don't sweat it. You know more without your notes than they'll learn from them. I've told you before. You're the smartest person in that courtroom when it comes to the science and medicine of this drug. No one knows more than you. There's no way they can touch you."

"Yeah, right." I felt particularly exposed as my mind piled up the negatives. Defense lawyers had my notes. Private jet or not, I still had a long plane ride home, and I had to be in the hospital by six the next morning to meet the family. I don't sleep well on planes, so I would have a maximum of four or five hours of sleep—if I could fall asleep at all. I felt guilty I wasn't there for the family when they arrived in Indy earlier in the day, and I would be under stress all day the next day making certain the procedure was done correctly.

When I realized the trial was going to go long, I asked my colleague—John Miller, a terrific electrophysiologist I had recruited when I was chief of cardiology, who would be doing the catheterization—to tell the family I was delayed but that everything was planned and in place. I would talk with them before the procedure started in the morning, answer any questions, and outline exactly what to expect. He said they seemed okay with that, but I still felt guilty.

Then, assuming it all went well, I had to fly back the next afternoon or evening, and be prepared to face Sam for a grueling five or six hours on the witness stand the day after that.

Damn it all!

While it was true I knew more science and medicine than Sam or his colleagues did, that was only a part of it. Trials are about winning, not about who knows more or (sadly) who is in the right. It's about showmanship as much as anything else—being able to convince a jury, often just high school-educated, about complex medical issues. I had to be a good showman as well as a believable doctor, scientist, and epidemiologist.

And Sam was good. He could attack my credibility in front of the jury in ways totally unrelated to what facts I knew or didn't know. The unpredictability of jury trials is what makes lawyers on both sides want to settle if possible. Too late for that.

I went back to the hotel, grabbed some clothes and a toothbrush from my room, and piled into the back of Bill's limo. Bill sat next to me, his arm across my shoulders. I think he didn't want to leave me alone so he could be sure I got on that plane.

I was so keyed up I couldn't sit still. I squirmed and fidgeted on that back seat and edged away from Bill's arm. Had I been driving, I'd have been stomping the accelerator to the floor and probably ticketed for speeding. The limo driver didn't rush, since the plane wouldn't leave without me. The ride to the airport seemed to take forever. I was a most unhappy camper.

Bill tried small talk to cut the silence, but I wasn't interested. I churned inside. All I could focus on was a very wealthy family traveling all the way from Saudi Arabia to have a procedure done in my institution, and me not being there until the morning of the procedure. And then coming back to face a well-prepared Sam out for blood—mine!

Pavarotti had it right. But this time, my angst wouldn't disappear when the curtain went up.

29

MY PATIENT

I must admit traveling by private plane is the only way to fly. It eased my burden somewhat and reminded me of a limerick Joan had once tacked on the refrigerator door:

Hush little luxury, don't you cry.
You'll be a necessity by and by.

The limo dropped me at the private terminal. I got out with my carry-on. A flight attendant met me and took my bag, and I boarded. The pilot came back to make sure I was comfortable and buckled in, and we took off. That was it. No lines, no security, and no hassle. If I ever win the lottery (or if one of my novels makes it to the *New York Times* best seller list), the first thing I'd change in my life would be to travel by private plane.

I arrived in Indianapolis at about eleven that night, exhausted. Bill had arranged a pickup at the airport, and I walked out of the plane and into the car. It took me straight home.

Joan was waiting for me, extra-dry Beefeater's gin martini in hand. Gordon had taught us well. We sat in the kitchen and talked. I was still so shaken I was near tears as I told her what I had been through, what I faced tomorrow and the next day. I unloaded about all the stress, and once again she questioned my sanity: why continue to accept medical legal work?

I have often thought that issue through. I've concluded—not to get too high and mighty—that it's like paying dues to live in the society we have, with all its warts. Certainly, I am well paid for what I do, but it's more than that. Someone with an important reputation needs to stand up and do what's right: defend the innocently accused or confront the wrongdoers. It's that simple. Many physicians frown on what I do and want no part of it, but I think expert testifying is a necessary duty. Without it, our legal system could not function. So, damn the naysayers.

I finished the martini and fell into bed after midnight. It was a rough night. The dreams were nonstop. One bizarre episode had me on the witness stand arguing with the Saudi patient's mother over her daughter's care.

Five o'clock in the morning came too quickly. I dressed and prepared an overnight bag. The car from the night before picked me up. The driver dropped me at the hospital and indicated he was on call to take me back to the airport whenever I was ready.

The Saudi family arrived shortly after I did. We spent an hour or more discussing the daughter's diagnosis. I took them through the procedure we'd be doing. As John Miller had reported, they were perfectly fine with everything, and the daughter was prepped for the catheterization.

Thank goodness, the procedure went textbook perfectly. The electrophysiology team's skills were incredible.

One of the EP doctors inserted a catheter into a blood vessel and navigated it to a precise place in her heart. We used a pacemaker to start her rapid heartbeat, determined where it was coming from, burned that area, and cured her of her problem. The whole procedure took barely two hours, start to finish. She was now a perfectly healthy sixteen-year-old, ready to return to her teenage life in Saudi Arabia with no medical restrictions and no fear of rapid heartbeats. I could not have wished for a better outcome. What a load off my mind! I felt exhilarated.

I spent another hour with the family afterward and once again reviewed the entire procedure and its outcome. Mother and patient were very happy. I told them I had to leave for a day but would like to see them when I returned, if they were still in town. The mother said they planned to shop for several days. They would see me when I got back.

Reluctantly, I had my secretary call the driver to come and get me, and the pilot to prepare the plane. I steeled myself to dive back into the courtroom battle.

30

BACK IN COURT

"Dr. Zipes, please remember you're still under oath," the judge cautioned the following morning as I slowly walked to the witness box and sat down.

"Yes, sir," I answered.

I felt like hell. I had stayed up late the night before after arriving at my hotel, prepping the science and epidemiology studies. It was one in the morning when I quit. Although exhausted, I had to take a sleeping pill to fall asleep. Not a good start to a long day. Sam was in attack mode and wasted no time coming after me, in my face again. He was so close I could see the blood vessels pounding in his neck and feel his breath on mine.

"Dr. Zipes, do you remember on direct questioning with your lawyer yesterday—oh, excuse me, two days ago. I forgot you asked for a day off, sorry about that. Did you take care of what was so urgent that you had to skip court?"

"Objection, Your Honor," Bill interrupted before I could answer. "None of this is relevant to the trial."

"Sustained," the judge said. "Counsel will confine his questions to the issues at hand."

"Yes, Your Honor," Sam said with a smile, having made his point to the jury. Now they all had to be wondering what was so important that I had wanted a day's grace from testifying.

"Two days ago, you quoted this article"—Sam held it up for me to see—"and you said, and here I am quoting you, 'It was a beautiful study.' Do you remember saying that?"

"Yes."

"Why was it a beautiful study, Dr. Zipes?"

"It was very well performed and analyzed scientifically."

"And the conclusions they reached agreed with your own opinion on how you think the drug should work, correct?"

Before I could answer, he cut me off with, "Why didn't you talk about studies that didn't agree with your opinions, Dr. Zipes, like this one?" He was going for my jugular, and I couldn't do much about it.

He turned and held out his hand, and the paralegal who'd copied my notes the other day handed him a cluster of papers.

"This study flat out disagrees with you. Does that make it an ugly study?" he said with a sneer. He waved the papers in front of my face.

"Your Honor, may Dr. Zipes see the study before commenting?" Bill asked the court.

"Of course. Counsel will give Dr. Zipes a copy of the study."

Sam handed it to me. Why hadn't I found this earlier? I had searched the web and the government site, PubMed, that listed all published papers about the drug. I must've seen it and discarded it because it had a flaw. I had read so many papers it was hard to keep track. This was an area that had been assigned to the epidemiologist. Sam might have found a hole in my argument, probably from analyzing my notes. I knew giving him a copy would come back to bite me.

My head was swimming, and my hand trembled as I took the paper from Sam. I felt all eyes of the jury on me.

"Take your time reading it," Bill called out.

"Your Honor, there's no question pending," Sam said. "I did not shout out during plaintiff's direct exam." He pointed a finger at Bill. "I would request the same courtesy," Sam added, an edge in his voice.

"Dr. Zipes, take the time you need to become acquainted with the paper," the judge said.

"Yes, Your Honor. Thank you."

I tried to focus on the ten pages of densely packed scientific information in front of me. On a good day, in the quiet of my office, it would take me at least ten or fifteen minutes to read and interpret the paper. Here, I was feeling lousy, tired, not thinking as sharp as I might, in a crowded courtroom with everyone staring at me, and I had to digest the paper's content. True, the judge said take all the time I needed, but there was no way they all were going to wait ten minutes for me to finish reading. I had about a minute to come up with an answer. Talk about stress! My palms were so wet the paper was sticking to them.

"So, Dr. Zipes," Sam said before I had finished reading, walking first in front of the jury to flash them a smile and then confronting me with hands on hips, "is this a beautiful paper that disagrees with your premise, or will you label it ugly"—it seemed like he pronounced it in three syllables, *uh-ga-ly*—"since it doesn't support your view?"

I tried not to panic as my eyes flew over the paper. I scanned the summary at the beginning of the article. As Sam stalked about, the flaw hit me, and I remembered why I had discarded it. It was my chance to take a swing at Sam.

I held the paper up and turned to the jury. I had to convince them, not Sam. The scientific argument was very intense, and they would be watching my body language, along with Sam's.

"All the patients in the study were young and healthy and therefore would not have been at risk from the drug," I said. "As I indicated two days ago, the drug is only harmful to those already at risk of heart attacks. The drug then pushes them over. These healthy subjects could take the drug without risk, at least for a while. They were not a proper group to test the drug's harmful effects." I tried to be as professorial as I could but in a helpful way—a teacher talking *with* students, not *down* to them. That would be a sure way to get them angry at me.

I turned back to look at Sam. "I don't know whether to call the paper beautiful or ugly, and I don't think we need to do either, but the results are completely consistent with my testimony earlier. If you remember, I said—"

"Thank you, Dr. Zipes, that's enough." Sam didn't bat an eye. A good lawyer never shows surprise or disappointment in front of a jury. "I'm sure we all remember what you said."

Bill was on his feet. "Objection, Your Honor. Counsel has to let the witness finish his answer."

The judge looked at me. "Dr. Zipes, do you wish to add anything more?"

I had made my point, but the judge was giving me room to hammer it home. "Just to emphasize that the negative outcome was anticipated from this study and cannot be used to challenge what I said earlier."

"Thank you," the judge said. He looked at Sam. "Counselor, you may continue."

Sam held his hand out to his defense table again. "What about this study, Dr. Zipes?" Unbidden, the same paralegal handed him another sheaf of papers. The defense team was well choreographed.

"The people in this study were elderly," Sam said, reading from the paper. "Average age sixty-five. Everyone had high blood pressure and high cholesterol and were clearly at risk of heart attacks. Yet none of them—I repeat," Sam said, now facing the jury and waving the papers dramatically, "*none*—had a problem taking the drug. No side effects in this vulnerable population, especially no heart attacks or strokes. Nobody was 'pushed over into a heart attack,' to use your words, Dr. Zipes. This study," he shook it in the air so the pages rattled, "totally defeats your argument, doesn't it, Dr. Zipes?"

Sam handed me the paper. "Take a look, Dr. Zipes. Another study that disagreed with you that you just happened to overlook and forgot to tell the jury about." Sam shook his head, assuming a disgusted expression.

"Well, Dr. Zipes," Sam asked impatiently after just a couple of minutes. "What do you think? Ready to give up your flawed conclusions based on this 'beautiful paper?'" Sam pronounced it *bea-u-ti-ful*. He paraded in front of the jury as if he had just won a decision for the defense.

I struggled. He was right. This population was at risk for heart attacks and should have shown side effects of the drug. A significant percentage should have had strokes and heart attacks. What had I missed?

I studied the paper. Again, I felt all eyes in the courtroom glued to my every move as I turned a page. I knew that most, if not all, of the jury didn't understand the details about which we were arguing. The issues were too complex. The jurors were interested in how Sam and I interacted to decide who they should believe, who was winning this verbal combat.

I reviewed the paper closely, my eyes traveling over the summary. What shortcomings had I seen? My mouth got dry, and my armpits wet. I looked up at Bill, but he couldn't help me. I took a sip of water to buy more time.

Then—I had it! There it was, all the time, and the reason I had ignored the paper in my report.

Sam walked toward me wearing that same smug look on his face. His body language—the way he moved, held his head, raised his eyebrows—telegraphed victory. He was eager to show the jury that he was smarter than I, smarter than all of them, that this Harvard and Duke-trained doctor didn't know what he was talking about.

From my notes, he knew which articles I had included, which I had rejected, and probably what my answers were going to be. And he had found my vulnerable underbelly—or so he thought—in the articles I had not discussed. But I think he didn't understand the science that well, so he was not discriminating in which articles he could use to try to make his point.

I kept my expression neutral, but my heart started to pound. This could be payback for all Sam's sarcasm and bullying. As he got closer, I couldn't help but think to myself, *Keep walking, you sonofabitch. I'm about to chop your head off.*

"Well, Dr. Zipes? No comment about this bea-u-ti-ful study that found no side effects even though the patients were at risk?"

I held the paper out to him. "Aspirin," I said and stopped.

I could see questions on the faces of the jurors. Everyone was anticipating an explanation, but I wanted Sam to pull it out of me. I wanted the jury to see that.

I glanced at Bill. He wore a wide smile. *He* knew where I was going. He understood the science.

"So they were taking aspirin. So what?" Sam asked, the smug look draining from his face. I think he anticipated something bad was going to happen to his argument.

"As I'm sure you remember from my direct testimony, Counselor, aspirin would block the drug's effects. All patients in the study were taking aspirin. They were protected from the harmful effects of this drug. Therefore, this *bea-u-ti-ful* study once again supports everything I said."

I couldn't help but add, "Thank you so much for calling my attention to it so I could share it with the jury." I turned to them and gave a slight nod.

I had landed a big blow, and did it feel good!

Sam was down but not out.

"One more question, Dr. Zipes. Did you practice your presentation with Harry Jones (not his real name)?"

"I don't know who Harry Jones is."

"You most certainly do, Dr. Zipes. He was sitting behind you just before you came to the witness stand and you were talking to him."

I had no idea what or who Sam was talking about. He seemed to be throwing a Hail Mary.

Sam spoke to his paralegal. "Put Jones's picture up." He was a bearded guy, mostly bald, with a prominent nose.

"Oh, that man," I said, when the image flashed on the screen. I recognized him from the war room. He was a professional who assessed and tutored witnesses. Bill had hired him to help prepare the witnesses for their testimony, but I had not worked with him. Sam was taking a long shot that this expert had prepped me in hopes that would weaken my testimony for the jury.

"No, I've not had any interactions with him, other than to say hello."

Despite all his experience, Sam seemed to crumble. My image was of Humpty Dumpty falling off the wall, his shattered eggshell draining yellow liquid yolk onto the sidewalk. Sam's face cracked; it showed disappointment, then anger.

"No more questions, Your Honor," Sam said in a clipped voice and sat down.

Whispers from the jurors breezed in the courtroom as they looked from me to Sam and then each other.

"Order. Order in the courtroom," said the judge, banging his gavel. "Counselor," he asked Bill, "any questions on redirect?"

"No, Your Honor," Bill said.

"Dr. Zipes, you are dismissed. Thank you for your testimony. The court will break for lunch and resume promptly at one thirty."

We rose as the jurors filed out. I left the witness chair and walked down the center aisle separating plaintiff and defense sides. Sam had his back to me. I thought I overheard him say to his paralegal, "I hate Bill, but I hate Zipes more."

Bill caught up with me outside the courtroom.

He beamed and gave me a hug. "I told you that you knew more than he did. That last exchange just won the case for us. Well done. Bea-u-ti-ful!"

I gave a short laugh, more of a snort. "Bill, you put me through hell. It damn well better be worth it."

"It was. You'll see. The jury will give us the verdict. Let's grab a quick lunch so we can get back to see who Sam puts on the stand. He's got to try and undo the damage."

"No," I said. "I'm done. Get me that plane, please. I'm heading back to Indy now."

"Don't you want to be here for the rest of the trial? Just a few more days. I can taste the victory already."

"I've had it with trials for now and for a long time to come. I want to get back to my patient. That's where I belong. You can email me the outcome."

I walked out of the courtroom, went back to my hotel, checked out, and collapsed with a sigh in the back of the limo. I dozed on the plane back home—a first for me—and felt the anxiety begin to drain. The tall, extra-dry Beefeater's gin martini—no olives or ice—helped.

167

That evening, my wife and I visited the Saudi family in their hotel suite. The daughter was feeling fine and bubbling over in anticipation of her new life, free from heart problems. At age sixteen, I suspected she would soon develop other issues of the heart.

The family had bought several sets of Louis Vuitton luggage to hold their many purchases. The suite was a bustling mix of people trying on new jeans, packing, and munching on a medley of fruit, Godiva chocolates, and nuts scattered about. They were preparing to leave the next day.

The mother sat serenely, puffing on her hookah. I didn't know until later that part of their shopping spree had been at a local jewelry store. Apparently, their limo had pulled up after closing hours and the store was dark. When the owner saw the limo and heard the chauffeur knocking at the door, he wisely reopened his shop. The mother purchased a *handful* of Rolex watches, which she distributed to key members of my EP team. She had also bought a Rolex for my wife similar to the Rolex the father had given me when I had made my house call months before.

This stressful period concluded with a fairy-tale ending. Bill called several days later. The jury had ruled in our favor and awarded the plaintiffs $51 million. Jurists said they hated that Sam was literally in my face during the trial. Defense appealed the decision, and the judge reduced the amount of the award. But a win was still a win.

The trial and my interactions with the lawyers profoundly affected me. I had already published my first novel, *The Black Widows*, and was looking for a topic for my second novel. I combined my experiences in this trial with testifying at one other trial, in which I defended a colleague from a malpractice charge, and fictionalized them into my second novel, *Ripples in Opperman's Pond*. The writing helped me work through the emotional trauma of the trial.

31

THE FBI, TASERS, AND THE DEPARTMENT OF JUSTICE

On September 12, 2001, the day after 9/11, the Federal Bureau of Investigation (FBI) had scheduled their first outreach program in Indianapolis to foster good relations with local communities. Citizen participation in this special liaison has provided mutual understanding, respect, and information about law enforcement. Through the FBI Citizen's Academy, community leaders have viewed firsthand the inner workings of the FBI, the issues they face, and how they tackle the problems.

I was part of a group of about thirty that joined the FBI Citizen's Academy the following year. We met at the FBI headquarters one evening a week for eight weeks, learned about various FBI projects and concerns, viewed a mock SWAT team takedown of five terrorists holding hostages, toured the FBI training facility in Quantico, Virginia, and had the opportunity to shoot multiple firearms at the training facility. My prior experience with my Red Ryder BB gun and Mossberg .22 earned me a coveted "Top Gun" rating. Our group elected me as president for that year.

One of the most exciting evenings we spent was listening to a lecture, followed by a discussion on the use of deadly force, when it could be used and in what form. To illustrate what FBI agents faced, they displayed a simulation video depicting real-life scenarios, gave us a handgun modified to shoot a laser beam, stood us in front of the screen, and said, "You're the special agent in charge (SAC). Your job is to arrest the suspect. What are you going to do?"

The instructor handed me the gun and rolled the film. I was suddenly transported to the entrance of a bank confronting a robber who pointed a gun at a bank teller. In a split second, I had to decide what to do. Facing the bank robber was so real my heart rate sped to 150 beats per minute; I was sweating and hyperventilating. I crouched, aimed my gun, and shouted, "FBI. Drop the gun and get down on the floor. Now!" The robber spun around and pointed his gun at me. I shot first. Replay showed my shot caught him flush in the chest. He collapsed on screen, dead.

My knees were weak as I looked at the instructor. "Good job," he said. "Want to try another?" I nodded, my heart still pounding, and turned back to the screen.

A very tall, muscular man emerged from deep in the shadows of a bedroom connected by a doorway to the living room where I stood. He was bare-chested and had no gun. My job was to arrest him.

"Hands up," I commanded.

He raised his hands high over his head and walked slowly across the bedroom rug toward me. "Stop and drop," I yelled, "to the floor, now!" I was ready to slip my finger into the trigger guard of the gun.

He kept walking toward me, but his hands were high, and I saw no weapon. He appeared nonthreatening and even had a slight smile on his face. My trigger finger twitched, but the lecture flashed through my mind and made it clear I couldn't use deadly force yet.

"Stop!" I yelled again, my heart quickening as he approached. *Too late!* When he passed through the doorway from the bedroom to the living room, his right hand jerked upward in a flash, grabbed a revolver concealed in the doorjamb over his head, and shot me before I could even get my finger to move.

The reality of the scene left me speechless. I handed the instructor my gun, shrugged helplessly, and sat back down.

In *The Black Widows,* my female protagonist, Frankie, interacts with that same simulation video. She learns to be proactive, not reactive; to watch the bad guy's hands at all times; to never let down her guard because response times measured in milliseconds determine whether she walks away or gets carried out in a body bag; and to shoot to kill when there is "probable cause to believe that the subject poses an imminent danger of death or serious physical injury to the agent." Writing that scene was so real to me, and fun to do, because I had lived through it with the FBI class.

I didn't realize then that my FBI experience in dealing with bad guys—I was always amazed that the FBI agents used the term "bad guys," and not "killer" or "robber" or "perp," as in so many detective novels—would come in handy several years later when I became involved as a plaintiff expert witness in TASER litigation and had to analyze scenes from police shootings.

TASER is an acronym that the weapon's inventor, John Cover, took from the title of the book *Tom Swift and His Electric Rifle* (**T**homas **A.** **S**wift's **E**lectric **R**ifle). The TASER is an electronic control device shaped like a handgun that shoots barbs at a resisting subject. Once the barbs make contact, the TASER delivers an electric charge over wires connected to the barbs, which produces pain and muscle contraction to incapacitate the subject and give law enforcement time to subdue him. Users can also discharge TASERs by pressing the weapon directly on the subject's body.

Two lawyers contacted me in 2007 to review information about a man who had received five TASER discharges of five seconds each in approximately forty-three seconds with the tip of the device pressed on his anterior chest. During delivery of the last shocks or shortly thereafter, the individual became unresponsive, was subsequently found to have no pulse or respiration, and died. At the time, TASER had published no warnings that the shock might cause cardiac arrest and death. I testified it had done just that to this person.

My first involvement triggered almost a decade of very tense legal battles as an expert witness against TASER Inc. As I've said, my reason for being an expert witness, noted earlier, was to support positions I thought were right, sometimes taking a stand others avoided. It was (and is) my opinion that a TASER shock discharging at 1,140 times per minute has the potential to capture the heartbeat, increase the heart rate to unsustainable levels, and cause cardiac arrest. The company denied that this could happen.

I offered no opinions about whether TASER use was good or bad, since I felt that decision rested with law enforcement experts, not a cardiologist. My goal was to educate TASER users that the TASER shock could kill, however infrequently, and suggest ways to reduce that risk.

TASER Inc. has a well-earned reputation for being fearsomely litigious. Their excellent legal team played hardball with each case from the get-go, sometimes frightening off lawyers, medical examiners, and expert witnesses. Company experts often concluded, and convinced multiple courts, that triggers other than the TASER shock caused the death. Excited delirium, a hyperagitated state with ambiguous diagnostic criteria and challengeable credibility, was a favorite defense.

The Heart Rhythm Society invited me in May 2009 to debate Patrick Tchou, a friend and respected electrophysiologist from Cleveland Clinic, about whether TASERs could cause fatal ventricular arrhythmias. Pat had been a TASER investigator in a 2006 animal study that showed the TASER shock could take over the normal heartbeat of a pig and make the heart beat faster. During the debate, I concluded that the issue was not *whether* the shock could cause fatal ventricular arrhythmias but how *often* it did this. Pat basically agreed, noting that the risks of death were extremely low. I also indicated that the company should issue warnings about potential cardiac effects.

Two TASER representatives in the audience strongly and vociferously disagreed with my conclusions. Yet four months later, in September 2009, TASER Inc. issued its first heart warning. The company recommended that users no longer shoot for the center of mass (previously the recommended target) but now should lower their sights to avoid chest shots if possible. Of course, they denied their warnings had anything to do with my statements at the debate.

TASER followed this warning two weeks later with a letter from Rick Guilbault, vice president of training, claiming that the reason for changing the target zone "has less to do with safety and more to do with effective risk management for law enforcement agencies." The letter went on to say that "the risk of VF is extremely rare and would be rounded to near zero." In my opinion, this letter greatly undermined the impact of the warning.

Among the many cases I reviewed was one sent to me by a lawyer, John Burton. It was of a seventeen-year-old lad who received a thirty-seven-second TASER shock to his chest, had cardiac arrest, and died.

The case went to a jury trial at which I testified. Toward the end of my testimony, the TASER defense attorney, John R. Maley, the most gracious of TASER's hardnosed litigation team, set forth a large stack of papers for the jury to see. He said something like, "Dr. Zipes, we've copied some of the eight hundred publications listed in your curriculum vitae." He placed his hand on the pile. "Have any of the papers you've published dealt with TASERs and any harm they might produce?"

That was an effective theatrical move since I hadn't published any TASER papers. It didn't sway the jury, however, which awarded plaintiff a $5 million judgment, later reduced on appeal.

But it got me thinking. None of the many publications on TASER concluded that it could kill by causing cardiac arrest. The closest was a 2005 letter to the editor published in the *New England Journal of Medicine* about a fourteen-year-old boy who received a seventeen-second TASER shock to his chest, lost consciousness, had ventricular fibrillation recorded by an ECG two minutes later, and was then resuscitated. I contacted the author for more information, but he begged off, saying essentially that TASER lawyers had already contacted him and he was too frightened to get involved.

I decided it was up to me to write the first paper to warn TASER users of the potential for sudden death. I collected eight cases I had reviewed over the years in which I concluded that TASER shocks had induced cardiac arrest (seven died). I published the case series in 2012 in *Circulation*, the leading clinical cardiology journal of the American Heart Association.

Before publication, I sought input from a lawyer specializing in libel litigation to be certain TASER had no grounds to sue me. His opinion was that "it is unlikely that a plaintiff would be successful" in making such a claim. Nevertheless, I took out libel insurance. While the claim might not be successful, legal fees defending my position could be substantial. Fortunately, no claim was ever filed.

I also sent the *completed* manuscript to two expert electrophysiologists and to the lawyer, John Burton, prior to publication, to make certain I had my facts correct, and to my wife for copyediting.

To say the paper caused an explosion would be an understatement. At my next deposition, TASER's chief counsel grilled me line by line, zeroing in on any inaccuracies. He found several misstatements that had no impact on my overall conclusions. He also asked for the critique of the paper by the *Circulation* editors prior to publication. I refused to provide this because such comments are confidential. I had to get the AHA's chief counsel to support my position because TASER wouldn't let up, demanding I produce the reviews.

After publication, a TASER representative wrote the editor of *Circulation* to allege that I had not written the paper, that a ghost author had done so, and that the journal should withdraw it. The editor was satisfied by my acknowledging that I had sent the paper for review to two electrophysiology experts, a lawyer, and my wife.

TASER's comments to the press were that I was a paid expert witness, implying that money influenced my writing and conclusions. I found the argument specious. If money was my goal, I would want to be involved in *more* cases, while my paper, by educating users, would result in *fewer* deaths and *less* cases.

My grilling at each new TASER case escalated. My wife teased that I'd better hire someone to start my car in the morning. Interrogation often took circuitous routes to undermine my credibility. In one deposition, we were seated at a long table with me at one end and a video reporter filming me at the other. A stenographer sat to my left, and the TASER lawyer at my right. The TASER lawyer, a relatively young man, pursued a line of inquiry that went something like this:

"Dr. Zipes, a biography about you was recently published in the *American Journal of Cardiology*."

"Yes," I answered.

"How did that come about?"

"I was interviewed by the editor of the journal, Bill Roberts, and he wrote the biography."

"Were you truthful during your interview?" the lawyer asked.

"To the best of my knowledge."

"The biography indicated you liked chemistry while at Dartmouth College and took eight chemistry courses."

"Yes."

"And that you got As in all eight."

"I think so. After all, it was many years ago."

"Well, Dr. Zipes, I've got a copy of your Dartmouth College transcript," he waved a paper in front of me, "and you only got five As."

While obviously a trivial issue, in front of a jury, that sounds like lying for self-promotion and begins to erode my credibility.

He continued.

"Dr. Zipes, you said you graduated cum laude."

"Yes," I said.

"For the benefit of the jury, what does that mean?"

"With honors."

"And you said that was the top 10 percent of the graduating class, correct?"

"I know I graduated cum laude, and I think that meant the top 10 percent."

"Your transcript," he again waved the paper in front of me, "indicates you were only in the top 13 percent."

I wanted to say, "Who gives a shit?" but of course I didn't. It's those kinds of shenanigans that make you hate lawyers and that keep many doctors from getting involved with them.

After my publication in *Circulation*, I began to review TASER-related deaths in which the medical examiner concluded the TASER played a substantial role in causing the cardiac arrest. That was a new development. Previously, medical examiners made that diagnosis infrequently, if at all. TASER apparently had sued two medical examiners who had made that diagnosis, and I think it frightened off any others from forming the same conclusion.

I became the go-to person for many TASER cases, either by lawyers or the press from all over the world. I turned down most, participating only in those cases where I was convinced TASER played a substantial contributing role in causing death.

In 2011, TASER published warnings in their educational material that used words and phrases very similar to those I had written in my reports and given in testimonies: that the TASER shock could cause capture (take over the intrinsic heartbeat) and changes in heart rate and rhythm, and produce cardiac arrest. TASER's chief counsel even estimated the risk of TASER-induced death as 1:100,000. I have no idea whether that's an accurate estimate, but the point is that TASER, Inc. appeared to have acknowledged the conclusions I had made in my 2009 debate: the question was not *whether* TASER can produce cardiac arrest but how *often* it happened.

I still receive frequent requests to serve as an expert witness in TASER-related deaths, but I have achieved my goal of getting warnings in place and educating users. I now turn down virtually all offers. It is a relief to close the chapter on this stressful part of my life.

Sometime in 2007 or 2008, I received a phone call from two lawyers in the United States Department of Justice. They explained that the DOJ was going to launch an investigation into abuses of implantable cardioverter defibrillator (ICD) treatments in patients. The ICD is a device like a large pacemaker (Vice President Cheney had one implanted while still in office) that monitors the heartbeat and delivers therapy to terminate abnormal fast heartbeats. A preliminary investigation had revealed that many ICDs had been implanted contrary to the guidelines of the National Coverage Determination of the Centers for Medicare and Medicaid Services (CMS). But before the lawyers began the official investigation, they wanted physician input. They had gotten my name during their preliminary investigations and after talking to a number of people. Would I help?

The request took me aback. The DOJ lawyers were asking me to help them investigate, and possibly testify against, my colleagues, my fellow electrophysiologists, my friends. They made it clear that Indianapolis hospitals, including my own, would be investigated like any others.

How could I do this? Should I do this?

Scenes from *The Godfather* and similar mafia movies ran through my mind. *Omerta*, a code of silence, was the honorable behavior. Snitches were not to be tolerated and, in fact, would be killed. While I didn't expect the latter, ostracism or at least anger from those I considered friends could be forthcoming.

The conversation ended with a request from the lawyers that they come to Indianapolis to meet with me and explain their case. I could agree to that much.

Jeffrey Dickstein and Amy Easton arrived a week or so later. He was tall and slim, she was shorter and lovely. Jeffrey was the talker, fast but precise as he led the conversation. She was his backup, the brains with the facts. He turned to her often for confirmation and details. They were a perfect team.

But most importantly, they *listened.* We sat down in my home office and talked at length. They wanted to get this right, not just to wield the power of the DOJ but to apply it in a way that protected patients above all, but also physicians who might have bent the implantation rules but for a good medical reason. They were out to nail those who truly and knowingly broke the rules, the egregious implanters. They hoped for settlements from involved hospitals but were prepared to go to court if necessary. Would I help them achieve these goals?

It took a bit of persuasion—which they were good at—and I agreed but under one condition: I wasn't going to do this alone. I suggested that we form a committee of experts, even invite major societies to join, such as the Heart Rhythm Society, the American College of Cardiology, and the American Heart Association. Jeffrey and Amy readily agreed, and I supplied them with a list of expert names to invite.

Jeffrey and Amy spent the next many months traveling around the United States to visit with and recruit potential committee members before launching the official investigation. They patiently met with us several times as a group, individually many more times, listened to us, and eventually formed a list of rules that allowed for some interpretation of CMS's original mandate. After CMS approved these regulations, they launched the investigation.

From 2010 until 2015, Jeffrey and Amy pursued the wrongdoers. Using an army of specially trained nurses, they reviewed thousands of charts from hundreds of hospitals, ferreting out the lawbreakers. I and other committee members received boxes and boxes of these charts summarized by the nurses for our final adjudication.

In October 2015, the DOJ announced that "The Department of Justice has reached 70 settlements involving 457 hospitals in 43 states for more than $250 million related to cardiac devices that were implanted in Medicare patients in violation of Medicare coverage requirements ..." In February 2016, the DOJ added that they had reached settlements with an additional fifty-one hospitals for more than $23 million. A desirable fallout from the investigation was a significant decline in abusive ICD implants.

In retrospect, my decision to join in this DOJ investigation was a wise choice. I think—particularly the way Jeffrey and Amy carried it out, with integrity and a high level of competence—we made an important contribution to cardiology and medicine in general. Together, we established a standard of investigation, adjudication, and decision-making that protected patients and physicians.

PART V

INDUSTRY

EARL BAKKEN

32

In 1975, I received an invitation from an engineer at Medtronic Inc., a medical device company, to visit their headquarters in Minneapolis. When I was there, several leaders at Medtronic asked me to help them write educational material about pacemakers. After the success of that endeavor, they asked me to become a consultant to the company.

I never had industry ties before, so I sought the opinion of several senior physicians. They advised not to get involved, that consulting for industry would negatively impact my academic credibility—"No, you can't" once again.

Damn the naysayers, I did it anyway. One of the things I am gratified in my career is that I consulted for Medtronic for thirty-five years, until 2010, and *not once* has anyone in academia challenged my integrity because of that relationship, nor has my industry association prevented me from becoming president or chair of a number of very important organizations—including the Heart Rhythm Society, the American College of Cardiology, and the American Board of Internal Medicine—or serving as editor in chief of seven cardiology journals, five of which I was the founding editor. I was careful to recuse myself when any potential conflicts arose.

Earl Bakken, founder, first CEO, and chairman of the board of Medtronic, is one of the world's genuine humanitarians—an honest-to-goodness good guy. Earl dedicated the mission of his company and his own personal resources to the benefit of the patient. I was fortunate to meet Earl shortly after starting to consult for Medtronic, and we have had a forty-year friendship. In addition to helping people worldwide, Earl has been a source of inspiration and support for me personally.

Author and Earl Bakken in Utrecht, around 1980.

In 1980, Earl and I shared a seat on a tour bus in Jerusalem where we were attending a cardiology meeting. I mentioned to him that the fast-growing specialty of cardiac electrophysiology needed a basic textbook for learners and practitioners. Would Medtronic sponsor such an effort if I were to lead it?

In a heartbeat, Earl's response was "Absolutely. Go for it."

Around the same time, Gordon Moe was retiring as head of the Masonic Medical Research Laboratory. José (Pepe) Jalife, a close friend who had also studied with Gordon several years after I did, suggested that we hold a retirement party for him. That clicked with me but with an additional spin. Why not have a retirement party to which we'd invite leaders in cardiac electrophysiology from around the world, with the requirement that they write and bring with them a chapter summarizing advances in their specific area? We'd then edit the chapters into a textbook.

I went to Earl. Would Medtronic support the symposium and book?

Earl gave the go-ahead, and Gordon enjoyed a unique retirement bash at the *Amelia Island International Symposium on Cardiac Arrhythmias* in May 1984. The meeting gave birth to our first textbook, *Cardiac Electrophysiology and Arrhythmias*, published by Grune & Stratton shortly after.

Attendees at Amelia Island Symposium, 1984

Author, Gordon Moe, José Jalife, Amelia Island, 1984

That book paved the way for the first edition of *Cardiac Electrophysiology: From Cell to Bedside*, published by Saunders in 1990.

Not resting on our laurels and still reveling in the success of the Amelia meeting, I asked Medtronic to support a second meeting, this time in Keystone, Colorado. Nancy Stephenson directed this 1993 symposium for Medtronic, which was a successful repeat of Amelia Island. Attendees came with chapters, and the second edition of *Cell to Bedside* followed in 1994.

Cardiac Electrophysiology: From Cell to Bedside lives on, alive and well, with the eighth edition just published by Elsevier. It continues to serve as a go-to reference source for heart rhythm experts around the world.

Earl, always interested in the totality of patient care, was a believer in alternative forms of medicine. Not just accepted modalities like yoga, acupuncture, meditation, dietary supplements, and the like—more fringe practices intrigued him, such as biofeedback, faith healing, and Portuguese surgery without cutting. He organized a symposium at a ranch out west for experts in each method to present their specialty. Earl invited me to serve as the scientific skeptic to judge the veracity of each discipline. I was eager to learn about new approaches to patient care and to potentially broaden my treatment horizons.

The meeting was life-changing. An hour of meditation kicked off each morning. I had never done this before, but I began hour-long meditation sessions with a skilled practitioner. I found this extremely relaxing and satisfying, and maintained it for several years until time crunches interfered and I could no longer squeeze it into my schedule.

I was privy to a panoply of health applications. Some, like the Portuguese surgery without incisions, I found to be a total hoax. The "surgeon" swabbed a "patient's" belly with an antiseptic, did a sleight of hand, and "pulled out" a piece of diseased liver without cutting the skin. The secret was an animal's liver hidden in the folds of the drape that materialized with a flourish of hand waving.

Other methods, such as mind-body interactions, produced unchallengeable outcomes that defied my understanding of physiology. For example, a university pediatrician who treated children with leukemia convinced the children to visualize "good" cells ridding the body of "bad." To prove the power of the brain, she had one youngster mentally raise his skin temperature higher than 100 degrees Fahrenheit, documented by a thermistor probe on his finger. How could that be with a core temperature of 98.6 degrees? I had no explanation. Another boy controlled his heart rate, making it rise and fall at will as documented by an electrocardiograph.

Two dramatic personal experiences also had no viable explanations.

The first evening, we all gathered in a room on the ranch where an expert in psychology engaged the group for over three hours. He drilled down into inhibitions and emotions buried deep in most of us, to rid ourselves of personal anxieties—fear, failures, shyness, embarrassments, whatever. Inspired by his talk, we shared personal feelings and, when the session ended, wrote our worst fear on a piece of paper. We went outside, gathered around a roaring fire, and tossed the paper into the flames, symbolically purging our fear. When the flames died down, he raked the glowing embers (1,400 degrees Fahrenheit) into a twelve- or fifteen-foot-long path.

"Whoever successfully jettisoned his fears can safely walk barefoot along this path without burning his feet," he said. "Your brain will provide a protective layer to your skin."

It sounded like a bunch of garbage, but at that point he had us (me) so pumped I'd have walked through a brick wall. I was first in line, bursting with eagerness. I faced the glowing embers, rubbed my bare feet back and forth like a bull waiting to charge, and trod over them without so much as a minor blister.

It turned out the three-hour psychological preparation didn't play a role. Joan, who had not been affected at all by the drama or preparation, and had stood quietly on the sidelines watching everyone else walk, at the last moment decided to give it a try. With encouragement from the group shouting for her to visualize "Cool moss, cool moss," she walked the embers, also without even redness to her feet. I have no explanation.

Earl and Doris, his wife, initially spectators with Joan, remained that way.

The second event occurred the following evening. In a different room with a different leader, we tried our hands at spoon bending. With a loud clang and clatter, the leader dumped a bag full of ordinary household silverware on the floor in the center of the room. We were all instructed to pick out a utensil. Then, with the group chanting in unison (I forget what we were chanting), we rubbed a point on the spoon or fork with our thumb. My spoon—as Ripley said, "Believe it or not"—got soft where I rubbed. I twisted the neck of the spoon into curlicues and bent in half the curved bowl portion of another spoon. Joan tried and failed until the leader came over and put his hand on her shoulder. Amazed, she watched the stem of the spoon bend. Crazy, yes?

But I have the spoons to prove it and have published pictures of them. Again, no explanation.

Author with bent spoons at alternative medicine symposium, around 1982.

Author's spoon bending.

At the end of the symposium, after evaluating all the presentations and my own experiences, I concluded there were three types of health care delivery: conventional that we are all used to, accept, and for which solid experimental support exists; frontier stuff that was real but for which I had no explanation; and clear hoaxes.

Earl retired from Medtronic in 1989 and built a home in the Kona District of Hawaii using only local workers and supplies. Once established in his new residence, he raised money for and founded the North Hawaii Community Hospital—the first hospital in the area. At age ninety-four, he still supports the hospital, which focuses on the patient with a "high-tech, high-touch" atmosphere.

Not all my experiences with Medtronic were so successful. In fact, two were downright dreadful. One of them almost got me fired, while the other one did.

33

THE INVENTION

In 1983, while consulting for Medtronic, I came up with the idea of delivering an electric shock over a catheter in the heart to terminate a rapid heartbeat. We called it the synchronous intravenous cardioverter. Medtronic engineers, with my input, wrote the patent application. I was listed as the sole inventor, but Medtronic was the assignee. Per my contract, all proceeds went to them, and I've never received a penny—Joan has reminded me many times that, while I might be a smart doctor, I'm a lousy businessman.

Medtronic built the device for me to test and implant in patients. Medtronic then fabricated the PCD, a pacemaker, cardioverter, and defibrillator combined into one device that incorporated my invention.

Around this time (late 1980s), I gave a lecture during which I said the PCD was the Rolls Royce of devices. A salesman for Eli Lilly, which sold their own version of the defibrillator via their company, Cardiac Pacemakers Inc. (CPI), took affront, reported what I'd said to his superiors, and triggered a maelstrom of legal controversy.

The CPI defibrillator was still under patent protection. Lilly sued Medtronic, claiming that Medtronic was "preselling" its PCD device and, in so doing, infringing on Lilly's patent protection. Judge John William Ditter of the United States District Court in Philadelphia decided in Lilly's favor and, in 1988, ordered Medtronic to cease its activities.

Since much of my own research at the time dealt with the cardioverter I had invented and the PCD that evolved from that invention, I refused to stop lecturing, publishing, and researching in this area. Lilly complained to Judge Ditter that I was violating the court's order. The court found Medtronic in contempt and ordered them to tell me to stop immediately.

Medtronic did so, but I refused.

Medtronic explained to the judge that I was a consultant, not an employee, and they could not control my actions. I think Judge Ditter was furious that, as a federal court judge, he could not order "No, you can't" and make it stick on a doctor in Indianapolis. He instructed Medtronic that he would control me through them.

He ordered Medtronic to fire me as a consultant immediately, to pay me no money either owed or in the future, to remove me as the principal investigator of the intravenous cardioverter and PCD study, to confiscate all related material and devices from my office, to sever all communications with me, and to make a public announcement of his order.

Medtronic had no choice but to comply. Their chief counsel, Ron Lund, called me and related the above in a thirty-second phone call, concluding with, "I can't talk to you any longer. Hire a lawyer." Medtronic posted notices in the company's mailroom and switchboard instructing that no one was to have communications with Dr. Zipes.

To say I was devastated would be an understatement. I was crushed to be so vilified publicly for defending what I thought was my right to work and lecture as I chose. I was not a party to the lawsuit between these two behemoths and had done nothing wrong—except to be caught in the middle. But Judge Ditter didn't see it that way. I had defied him. First Amendment rights? Forget them. I had defied a powerful federal court judge.

I had to fight back tears when the Medtronic representative, accompanied by a law enforcement officer, came into my hospital office to remove all educational material—some of which I had written—about the transvenous cardioverter and PCD.

I had never felt so despondent in my life—before or since. I had trouble eating, sleeping, and concentrating on work. I'm sure I was a bear to live with. Joan did what she could to cheer me up, but I felt I had ruined my career by resisting the court's *no, you can't* order, even though I knew I was doing the right thing. I intended to stick to my guns.

At a national heart meeting of the American College of Cardiology the following month, a physician colleague, Arjun Sharma from Canada, presented material on the transvenous cardioverter to a gathering of about a thousand cardiologists. He started his lecture with a slide that had a picture of me with a red circle around my face and a red diagonal line across it, "No Smoking" style. I'm sure he thought he was being funny, but I didn't. He followed this with a slide of the order from the court and said, "If this person is in the audience, he has to leave because the judge said he cannot hear any material related to the topic I'm about to present."

I was in the audience, and I'm sure my ears turned red when I heard Arjun. I rose from my seat, walked deliberately to a microphone, and said, "That person is here, and he is leaving." I stomped out of the lecture hall, livid at what I perceived as a personal affront.

The next months of legal agony and ostracism were horrific. My reputation and integrity were more important to me than any worldly acquisitions or accomplishments, and I was devastated. I was forced to justify my actions to the dean of the medical school to avoid university reprimand, and to hire a lawyer to defend my First Amendment rights. (The lawyer was superb and helped write an amicus curiae brief—friend of the court document—in which she stated where once I was considered a paragon in the classroom, I was now a pariah. She could have been a novelist.) At heart meetings, my Medtronic colleagues were compelled to shun me. And they did, literally turning their backs, except for their CEO at the time, Win Wallin. Win dared disobey the court, put his arm across my shoulders, and reassured me all would work out.

Added to the stress was that, at the time, I was president of the North American Society of Pacing and Electrophysiology (NASPE, now called the Heart Rhythm Society), the largest group of heart rhythm experts in the world. Leading this important society when all its members knew their president was in legal difficulties was a challenge.

Judge Ditter's court order began to unravel because one of the patients in the transvenous cardioverter study was a federal judge. When he heard I could no longer take care of him, he called Judge Ditter and insisted I remain his doctor. Judge Ditter relented. Then, when other patients heard about this exception, they also demanded that I remain their doctor. Finally, when a device malfunctioned and no one could reprogram it correctly, I took over and—defying the court's contempt order to have no patient contact whatsoever—fixed the malfunction and saved the patient. (The lead character in my second novel, *Ripples in Opperman's Pond,* does the same thing. As with penning *The Black Widows,* writing that scene helped me work through my emotions.)

Medtronic appealed the court's decision. Almost a year after it all started, the US Court of Appeals for the Third District heard the case and reversed Judge Ditter's decision, ruling that Medtronic's actions did not infringe on the patent. I was vindicated and welcomed back to Medtronic with open arms. They gave me a picture of a Rolls Royce with the license plate "PCD" that hangs in my home today.

Lilly, not satisfied, took the case to the United States Supreme Court. In June 1990, Justice Antonin Scalia (now deceased) delivered the opinion of a 6–2 majority that upheld the appellate court's decision, ending the ordeal.

The episode struck home the immense power of the courts, especially a federal court and a federal judge, and the helplessness of the victim. What if I hadn't had Medtronic to press the case on to the appellate court, and then support the challenge to the Supreme Court? What if I hadn't been able to afford my own lawyer? What if I hadn't the confidence to fight Judge Ditter? The average working American stands little chance in such a legal system that says to him or her, "No, you can't."

The second Medtronic episode *almost* got me fired but was worth the trauma and four dozen red roses.

I have cochaired a symposium called Cardiostim in Nice, France, every other year since 1984. More than five thousand cardiologists and other health care workers from all over the world attend. Medtronic has always been a big supporter of the conference and a major presence. In the late 1990s, they planned a dinner for a large group of doctors and spouses attending Cardiostim at a restaurant known for a somewhat rowdy atmosphere and blaring wild music. Waiters served food family style on large platters to groups sitting together at long wooden tables. They refilled jugs of wine like water. Wine glasses after use crashed into a large brick fireplace.

Many of us had gathered at the Negresco Hotel to board a bus to the restaurant. When Nancy Stephenson, in charge of physician affairs for Medtronic, heard the bus would be late, she steered us into the bar to await its arrival. What do you do in a bar? You drink. So we did.

I was standing next to a charming and lovely woman who was lamenting the fact that her father was retiring and pressing her to take over the family business.

"What's the big deal?" I asked.

She responded that it was a multibillion-dollar family business—yes, with a B—and she wasn't sure she wanted to do it. We chatted a bit more, and when the bus finally arrived, most of us were pleasantly lubricated.

Frankly, I don't remember a lot of the evening after that. I do remember just finishing my dinner when a flying potato hit me in the forehead. Yes, a food fight—among distinguished but inebriated cardiologists—that I did not start but could not let go unchallenged. From throwing food to spilling red wine on lots of people—"Doug, not on my Escada blouse. Please!"—the affair degenerated into a boisterous but fun evening. I danced a lot and severely twisted my ankle on the wine-soaked dance floor (but didn't feel the pain until the next morning).

I found out later that the lovely billionaire lady was the wife of a senior Medtronic executive who had observed the event cold sober. That executive turned to the CEO—Bill George at the time—and said, "Bill, I want Zipes fired. His behavior is outrageous."

Fortunately, Bill forgave my errant conduct and just took the wine jug from my hand before we boarded the bus back to the Negresco. The next morning, after soaking my balloon-sized ankle in ice, I sent a dozen red roses to the billionaire, to Nancy, and to two other women I had doused with red wine. They all forgave me most graciously and laughed at the memory of an unforgettable evening, which became immortalized in the annals of Medtronic.

Several years later, I was being installed as the president of the American College of Cardiology. Bill George hosted a celebratory dinner for me. After dinner, we drove to the convention center for my installation.

I said to Bill, "I bet someone will comment about red wine."

Bill assured me that was all history and wouldn't happen. As soon as I exited the limo, a passing cardiologist said, "Hi, Mr. President Elect. No red wine for you tonight!"

When I retired as director of cardiology at Indiana University School of Medicine and the Krannert Institute of Cardiology in 2004, Nancy Stephenson arranged a magnificent party for me at the Negresco Hotel after the Nice meeting—so lavish it outshone Amelia and Keystone years before. I drank only two glasses—maybe three—of red wine the entire evening!

On my retirement from consulting for Medtronic in 2010, in addition to endowing a chair at Indiana University in my name, the company gave me a large granite cornerstone with the PCD embedded, symbolizing that my invention laid the groundwork for Medtronic's transition to treating rapid heart rhythm problems, now a multibillion-dollar initiative.

At the height of my consulting for the company, I traveled to Minneapolis four or six times a year. I usually stayed overnight at the Grand Hotel in downtown Minneapolis. It soon became like a second home to me.

During one trip, my host—Ed Duffin, one of the best and brightest at Medtronic, and a dear friend of many years, unfortunately deceased prematurely—took me to a late dinner. When we finished, Ed dropped me off at the hotel, and we arranged to meet the following morning.

I checked in at the front desk, got my room key, and took the elevator to the fourth floor. After performing the usual ablutions, I retired for the night. The room was warm, and I slept in my blue-striped boxer briefs.

Several hours later, I woke to use the bathroom. Half-asleep and feeling quite at home in this hotel, I didn't bother turning on the light. I opened the door to what I thought was the bathroom and allowed the door to close behind me—which it did with a loud *click*. That was when I realized I was not in the bathroom but standing out in the hall—in my undershorts—without my room key—at three in the morning!

Oh my God. What should I do? I looked for a phone in the hallway, present in many hotels. None.

I don't usually carry my cell phone in my underwear, so that was not an option.

I had no choice but to go downstairs to the front desk in the main lobby to get another key. I didn't know what I'd do if the clerk behind the desk asked for identification—or if the clerk was a woman.

The Grand Hotel is a very large and busy hotel. Even at three in the morning, there could be people checking in or checking out. Maybe they'd want to use the elevator. Whatever, it was not likely I'd be alone.

I got into the elevator and pushed the "lobby" button. When I reached the lobby level, I peeked out the door. Sure enough, a small crowd—airline folks, I thought—crowded around the check-in desk. I didn't know what to do. I certainly wasn't going to waltz across the floor to the front desk in my blue-striped undies.

I whistled. Yes, I whistled—a piercing, high-pitched, two-finger blast that I let go with full lung power. Then I ducked back into the elevator, prevented the door from fully closing, and used it as a shield.

The startled crowd looked all around to see who was making that racket. I was interested in just one guy—the bellhop. He was standing to the side of the check-in desk, ready to transport luggage for the newcomers. When he looked in the direction of the elevator, I flashed my bare arm in a "come here" motion.

The bellhop hurried over to the elevator. When he saw me, he began to laugh—not just a little chortle but huge, loud guffaws. He couldn't contain himself and had to lean against the elevator door for support. I thought he might double over onto the floor.

His behavior triggered looks from the crowd at the check-in desk, and several started to walk over to see what was so funny. Two of the group were female flight attendants.

Before they got too close, I grabbed the bellhop by the front of his shirt, dragged him into the elevator, and pushed the "close door" button. Then I hit the button to the fourth floor and ... we didn't move. Someone outside the elevator must've depressed the "up" button at the same time because the elevator door started to reopen.

I hit the "close door" button, but it wouldn't override the open command. I pulled the bellhop in front of me and hid as best I could behind him as the elevator door opened fully. I snuck out a hand to hit the "close door" button, and, fortunately, the door responded. I pushed the fourth-floor button, and the elevator rose. Thank goodness.

As we stood in front of the door to my room, the bellhop, still laughing, asked, "How do I know this is your room?"

"Open the damn door, and I'll show you my wallet," I said. "Hurry up. I'm freezing my butt off."

"Just kidding," he said, using his pass key to open the door. "Have a good night—and thanks for the entertainment." He strolled down the hall, laughing. "Man, do I have a story to tell tomorrow," I heard him say as I closed my door.

Thirty-five years after defying the naysayers about consulting for industry, I look back at my relationship with Medtronic as one of the highlights of my professional career. I interacted with bright people who cared about creating innovative, reliable products that helped patients, a heritage Earl Bakken established when he founded the company and passed down to the generations that followed him.

PART VI

ORGANIZATIONS

BECOMING A LEADER

Becoming president of the American College of Cardiology in March 2001 was one of the highlights of my career as I prepared to help lead that august organization (now more than fifty thousand members strong) into new challenges of incorporation, communication, education, and advocacy. George Beller preceded me as president, and when his wife became ill with cancer, he asked me to assume all his travel obligations. So, for two years, first as president-elect and then as president of the ACC, I traveled extensively around the world.

Author and Joan at ACC President's Reception, 2001.

Author as president of ACC, 2001.

Because more than fifty ACC presidents preceded me, and untold numbers would follow, I wanted to make my installation something different.

In the late 1990s, Joan and I received an invitation to attend a Dartmouth Medical School graduation from the medical school dean, Andrew Wallace—with whom I published my first paper thirty years earlier when we were both at Duke—to inaugurate a prize I had endowed for the best research performed by a graduating medical student.

Graduation day on the lawn of the medical school was bright and sunny. After the graduates had all received their diplomas and one had received the first Zipes Research Prize, a booming, mellifluous baritone floated from the back row of chairs. We turned to see a tall, broad-shouldered man approach. He was draped in a full-length white toga. A garland of laurel leaves surrounded his curly gray hair. He wore brown sandals, carried a long wooden staff, and walked toward us reciting the Hippocratic oath in Greek.

It was Hippocrates! I could picture this ageless physician, the father of modern medicine, walking the fields of ancient Greece hundreds of years before Christ, educating his disciples.

John Rassias, a well-known and distinguished language professor at

Dartmouth, then switched to English. He had the newly minted doctors on stage and the rest of us in the audience recite the oath after him. It was a marvelous reenactment and reaffirmation of our commitment to the ideals of the Hippocratic oath and to patient care.

That's what I'll do at my ACC presidential installation, I thought. *What could be better than having Hippocrates present?*

I called John several weeks later. He said he was interested, but March was exam week and he didn't think he could make it. During follow-up calls, he hemmed and hawed and wouldn't commit. I prevailed on Andy Wallace to talk to John. After much wrangling, John agreed to come. The ACC arranged for a costume shop in Orlando to provide his Hippocratic accoutrements, and everything was in place. The ACC staff was excited at this new twist to the memorable evening. I kept this surprise secret from everyone else.

I prepared my presidential address with initial comments focused on the meaning of the Hippocratic oath. My closing ended with, "And here comes Hippocrates himself," at which point John would walk in from the back of this huge auditorium and perform as he had at Dartmouth.

During the executive committee meeting two days before my inauguration, the chief administrator at the Mary Hitchcock Hospital in Hanover, New Hampshire, called.

"Professor Rassias has just been admitted with a mild heart attack and will be unable to travel to Orlando. He sends his regrets."

Oh my God. Now what was I to do? For a nanosecond, I considered dressing as Hippocrates but discarded that idea as ludicrous. No way could I pull that off. Since the hour was too late to change my talk substantially, I decided the best course was for me to recite an abbreviated version of the Hippocratic oath—the original is quite long and contains many portions no longer relevant—and have the physicians join responsively.

And that's what we did. What could have been a unique and unforgettable inauguration metamorphosed into an ordinary installation I'm sure most have forgotten.

Most but apparently not all. Recently a cardiologist contacted me to say he uses my inauguration speech—in which I said in part "treat each day as if it were your last and each patient as if he were your first" (a phrase Joan coined)—for incoming students and staff. So, part of that lives on.

Sadly, John Rassias died in 2015.

The morning after I became ACC president, I met the real president.

George W. Bush decided to unveil his plan for a patient's bill of rights at our national ACC meeting. He chose our venue to lay out his proposal to twenty-five thousand health care workers. Backstage, I was at the head of a receiving line as the president's limo rolled up. I had to pinch myself when the president of the United States stepped out of "The Beast" and walked toward me.

I held out my hand. "Good morning, Mr. President. I'm Doug Zipes and only became president of the American College of Cardiology last night."

"Good morning, Doug," POTUS said. "I only became president of the United States a few months ago. I'm sure we both have a lot to learn."

To Douglas Zipes
With Best Wishes,

*Author as president of ACC, meeting President George W.
Bush, 2001, with past ACC president George Beller.*

A few months later, I was part of a group that met with Bush in Washington to discuss the patient's bill of rights, along with another weighty issue, the use of fetal tissue for stem cell research. He promoted the former but vetoed the latter.

Then 9/11 came crashing down on the nation, and all priorities shifted. As president, I suggested the ACC respond with a donation to help buy a new ambulance for New York City. The German Cardiac Society joined with us to make the gift possible. We presented that to Mayor Rudy Giuliani at a ceremony the week after the disaster.

Walking near Ground Zero days after the disaster triggered images of what Pompeii and Herculaneum must have looked like after Mount Vesuvius erupted: eerie silence; dust in the air so thick it blanketed everything with a gray, sinister coating; a few ghostlike people walking about. One of my most gripping memories is of a pair of debris-covered women's shoes—its red color barely detectible—lying twisted, broken heeled, and abandoned in the middle of the road. *Who was she and what happened to her?* I wondered.

As president, I made many trips to ACC headquarters in Bethesda, Maryland. I would fly into Reagan National Airport in Washington, DC, and then taxi to Bethesda. I did this almost weekly until one winter night.

I took a late flight to DC that night. The taxi line seemed to stretch forever, and I was shivering, waiting for my turn. I had left my bulky overcoat home, figuring I would be outside only minutes. A cab pulled up at last, and by that time, my teeth were chattering. I handed the driver my wheelie carry-on and briefcase and piled into the back seat as he put them in the trunk. I told him where I wanted to go and to turn up the heat, and I settled in for the forty-five-minute ride to the hotel.

When we hit the George Washington Memorial Parkway, the driver looked at me in the rearview mirror.

"You tired?" he asked.

"I am."

"How about I turn off the radio and you lean back and sleep until we get to Bethesda?"

"Great," I said. I closed my eyes and began to doze. After a few minutes, I felt the cab slow, and I bolted upright.

"What's going on?" I asked.

"The battery indicator light's flashing, and I'll have to stop," the driver said, pointing to a flickering light on the dashboard. "Dead battery."

"Don't. Keep driving as long as the motor's running. Key Bridge to downtown DC is just ahead."

He ignored me and turned off onto a dark, bumpy road that expanded into an alcove of trees near a small parking lot. Moonlight glinted silvery off the surface of the Potomac River flowing alongside the parking lot. The area was deserted.

My heart began to pound. This was a mugging in the making, and I knew I was in big trouble.

I reached for my cell phone to call 911 but came up empty. The phone was in my briefcase in the trunk of the car.

The driver stopped the cab, flicked the headlights on and off twice, and blew the horn twice. So much for a dead battery. Then he got out of the cab, opened the hood, and I saw a shower of sparks as he disconnected the battery cable. He got back into the car, turned the ignition key, and the car motor just groaned.

"See," he said, "battery's dead like I told you. Just sit back and relax until roadside assistance comes. I called them."

Sure, I thought, *just wait for your buddies to show up.*

I jumped out of the cab. He got out also. "Where you going?" he asked, blocking my way. "I told you to wait in the cab."

My mind was racing. I didn't know what to do. One thing was certain: I wasn't going to hang around here. But I had important stuff in the trunk.

"Open the trunk. I want my things."

I'm not very big, but he was smaller, no more than five feet two or three and skinny. He just stood there, blinking at me.

"Open the trunk now, or I'll beat your bloody head in," I screamed, raising a fist and leaning into his face.

In retrospect, it's hard to believe a sixty-two-year-old (at the time) cardiologist even in reasonable shape, would do what I did, but desperate times make for desperate actions. My threatening behavior was enough to intimidate him, and he opened the trunk of the cab. I grabbed my wheelie and briefcase and tore out of the parking lot.

I ran toward the parkway, hauling the bouncing wheelie with one hand and clutching my briefcase with the other. The wheelie hit a stone in the road and tipped onto its side. I didn't slow to set it right and just dragged it along the gravel. I debated stopping to call 911 but figured the best thing to do was to get the hell out of the dark parking lot as quickly as possible.

I reached the parkway, held out my thumb, and waved at passing cars, trying to hitch a ride. I was wearing a jacket and tie, but it was late at night, and cars just whizzed by. No driver was about to pick up a lunatic waving from the side of the road at eleven o'clock, no matter how he was dressed.

I glanced back at the parking lot. Car lights flicked on, and the cab advanced slowly toward where I was standing. Traffic was too dense to run across the road, but the cab would find me if I stayed where I was.

Bushes lined the side of the highway. I yanked the wheelie and ducked behind one as the cab rolled by. It appeared that two people now sat in the front seat. I stayed hidden and watched the tail lights until they disappeared in the dark around a bend.

In the distance, I could see the lights of Key Bridge spanning the highway to downtown Washington. I ran alongside the road toward it, the wheelie bumping along on the grass.

When the traffic thinned, I darted across the pavement, bounced the wheelie over the curb and grass island divider, ran across the lanes traveling in the opposite direction, and climbed up a steep grassy embankment leading to Key Bridge. My foot slipped once in the wet grass, and the wheelie and I almost tumbled back down onto the highway.

When I reached the top, I leaned against the concrete side of the bridge to catch my breath. I was shivering again but not from the cold.

Heavy traffic crisscrossed the bridge into Washington. I spotted a cab, hailed it down, and jumped in, dragging the wheelie after me. The driver turned around and gave me a stare, eyebrows bunched.

"I could put that in the trunk if you want," he said.

"Just drive. To Bethesda as quickly as possible."

After a while, I calmed down and told him what had happened.

"Did you get the number of the cab?" he asked.

"No."

"License plate?"

"No."

"Then there's not much you can do. These things happen. Don't ever get into a cab without your cell phone to call 911."

Sage advice I've followed ever since.

ACC leadership was aghast when I related the story the next day. For the rest of my presidency, they sent a car to pick me up at the airport.

When I stepped down as president of the ACC in March 2002, I told the convocation audience a story that helped keep me focused on reality:

May is Race Month in Indianapolis as the city gets ready for 350,000 fans attending the Indianapolis 500, held on the Sunday before Memorial Day. The hotels fill, the restaurants are jammed, streets near the track resemble parking lots, and the entire downtown atmosphere becomes electrified in anticipation of the "greatest spectacle in racing."

It was early May a few years after we moved to Indy when I received a late-night call at home from a physician in a distant state. My career was just beginning, but I had been publishing a steady stream of research and clinical papers. So, while I was a relative youngster, my name had been in the medical literature with some frequency.

The doctor told me he was the family physician of a very prominent racecar driver whose mother got so excited when her son won the Indy

500 she developed atrial fibrillation in Gasoline Alley at the track. She had hypertrophic cardiomyopathy, a disease of the heart muscle, and the atrial fibrillation caused her to black out. The doctor wanted to know if I would be at the upcoming race to take care of her in case she had another spell. I assured him I would be there and would be happy to care for her.

At breakfast the following morning, I told my children, who were about ten, twelve, and thirteen, about the phone call. They were suitably impressed and concluded that perhaps their father might amount to an important doctor after all. (The driver didn't win, his mother didn't black out, and I was not needed.)

Fast-forward twenty-five or so years. I received another late-night call at home, this time from a very prominent NFL football player. He had suffered several near blackouts, and his doctor said the cause was a rapid heart rhythm called atrial flutter (first cousin to atrial fibrillation). His doctor recommended an ablation, a heart catheterization procedure to locate the site of the atrial flutter and burn that area to cure him of the problem (similar to what the Saudi patient underwent). The doctor had suggested the player call me to discuss it. The football player wanted to know what I thought and whether he should do as his doctor suggested.

We considered the pros and cons. I agreed with the doctor and suggested he have the ablation. Shortly after that, he did, and it eliminated the atrial flutter.

Now, anticipating history would repeat itself, I called my grandson Tyler, aged about ten. He was an avid sports enthusiast, and I knew he would recognize the football player's name instantly.

"Tyler, guess who called Papa last night?"

"Who, Papa?" Tyler asked.

I told him. There was a lengthy pause in the conversation. I could picture Tyler's face, eyes getting big and eyebrows raised, proud of his grandfather.

"Papa," Tyler finally said.

"What?" I asked.

"Did he have the wrong number?"

So much for trying to impress grandchildren. To Tyler, I am just Papa. It's better that way.

In 1989, the American Board of Internal Medicine invited me to join their cardiovascular board. At the time, the ABIM was one of the most prestigious organizations in internal medicine, charged with certifying all the subspecialties. To be officially called a cardiologist, a pulmonologist, a nephrologist, and so forth, one had to pass the ABIM's certifying examination in that specialty. Becoming a member of this organization was an honor and a highlight in my career.

After I joined, the board decided it was time to create a subspecialty in clinical cardiac electrophysiology (CCEP) and asked me to write the application for approval by the American Board of Medical Specialties. The ABMS rejected my first attempt, wrongly finding there was an insufficient body of cognitive knowledge to support a subspecialty in CCEP.

I rewrote the application, and the ABMS approved it. ABIM leadership asked me to chair the CCEP and direct the writing of its first and subsequent two examinations. After six years chairing CCEP, I then chaired the cardiology board for four, became a member of the overall ABIM board, and, in 2002 when I finished my presidency of the ACC, became the chairman of the board of the ABIM.

I had some misgivings about assuming this role because I felt it called for more right-brain leadership than I could provide. The ABIM board wrestled with wide-ranging and fundamental issues confronting medicine, such as new approaches to educating medical students, how to provide widespread health care, how to reduce medical errors, and how to reduce escalating health costs. At that level, the ABIM was a deliberative organization considering very weighty issues and was jokingly accused of "biting off *less* than it can chew," since it often discussed these issues ad nauseam without resolution. The board called them "big, hairy, audacious goals." They dropped the "hairy" part when someone raised the possibility it might be insulting to hirsute people.

I was my own naysayer but accepted the chair anyway. I had a successful tenure, working closely with Harry Kimball, president of the ABIM. We instituted the concept of maintenance of certification in cardiology, the idea that passing the initial certifying examination was just the beginning of a lifelong learning experience and certification in medicine and its subspecialties.

In 2004, at the request of members of the Israel Heart Society, I founded the Friends of the Israel Heart Society (FIHS), a not-for-profit international organization to help combat anti-Semitism in academic circles and support the IHS. Leading cardiologists worldwide joined, and we worked hard at our stated mission.

Richard Meltzer, a senior US cardiologist, made the first financial donation to the FIHS in memory of his parents. We invested the money in Israel Bonds. The FIHS has given the annual interest each year as a prize to an outstanding Israeli cardiologist selected by the IHS. For several years, we also supported a cardiology fellowship at Indiana University School of Medicine for an aspiring young Israeli doctor.

The organization has flourished. In 2009, I passed the reins to Jeffrey Goldberger, the current president. Jeff has expanded the base and raised money to send young cardiologists from the United States to attend scientific meetings in Israel.

I had a second goal in mind when I began the FIHS. I wanted to create an international symposium to which I would invite cardiologists from *every* Middle East country. I wanted a venue that would put Muslim, Christian, and Jew in the same room to discuss medicine and their patients. I hoped we would be able to bypass cultural, geographic, and religious barriers by focusing on our common enemy: cardiovascular diseases.

Author with camel in Qatar, around 2014.

Miep Gies, the woman who helped hide Anne Frank and the others in an Amsterdam attic during WWII, said ordinary people "can within their own small way turn on a small light in a dark room." That is what I hoped to accomplish, realizing how small the light and how big the room, but with a more expansive future goal that if everyone turned on a small light, the room would no longer be dark.

I found a generous benefactor in Indianapolis to fund the first meeting in 2009. It was a major success, with cardiologists attending from most of the Middle East countries. At dinner the first night, my heart did a gentle flip as I watched Israeli cardiologists eat and drink alongside Iranians; Egyptians next to Saudis; and so forth. We realized that when we looked each other in the eye, sans artificial barriers, we all cared about the same things: family, health, education, children, and our patients. While our skin may be different and we may pray to a god called by different names, we are all the same inside.

To expand the program, I asked the American College of Cardiology to take it over. They made it a focus of their outreach educational program. I directed the symposium for several more years and then passed it to the ACC completely. I had some money left over from the first meeting, which I transferred to the ACC. We have used it to fund a monetary award and a certificate for the Middle East cardiologists with the highest-ranked abstracts. The Ninth Middle East Cardiovascular Symposium was held in Washington, DC, in March 2017 and was considered "one of the most important educational endeavors of the College."

One of my passions outside medicine is opera. Not just any opera but Italian opera or—as I've often said—an opera composed by anyone whose surname ended in a vowel (Bizet and Offenbach are exceptions).

I became president of Indianapolis Opera in 1983. The company, founded in 1975, was in the middle of a major financial crisis. Presenting four operas a year with one performance Friday night and another Sunday afternoon was breaking our budget. Opera, with the cost of sets, costumes, orchestra, singers, and supporting personnel, is one of the most expensive art forms to produce. I soon realized that ticket sales—even with a full house—covered less than a third of our expenses. We had to raise the rest of the money by grants and individual donations.

Often, during my two years as president, the manager would seek me out after the Friday night performance to tell me that our coffers were empty. We had no money to pay for the Sunday performance. I felt that cancelling a single performance would spell our demise, so I would write a substantial check as a personal loan to the opera to tide us over.

Members of the opera board came up with a money-raising scheme that led to my one and only personal opera review. They suggested I take the stage after the first act of the opera and make a pitch to the audience to encourage contributions. In essence, to pass the plate for donations.

I agreed. Having lectured to large and small audiences around the world by that time, I didn't think I'd have a problem making a short presentation to the opera audience.

Big misjudgment. As I gazed out at a sea of tuxedos and gowns—the opera attire at the time—I realized I was way out of my comfort zone. I couldn't ask for my first slide, the audience was not physicians and scientists, and many of them knew far more about opera than I did. My heart pounded against my ribs, I was breathing rapidly, and my forehead was dotted with moisture.

I managed to make my pitch and raised about $10,000 that night. The reporter for the *Indianapolis Star* wrote a review of the opera performance in the Saturday morning edition. The article said something like, "Indianapolis Opera's performance of *Otello* was spectacular, and Dr. Zipes's presentation, though tacky, was necessary."

So much for my opera debut.

We were fortunate to have Luciano Pavarotti perform on January 28, 1986. It was a terribly sad day for all of America because the *Challenger* blew up that morning. But in true fashion that "the show must go on," after a moment of silence at the beginning of the concert, the tenor opened that evening with "Questa o Quella" from *Rigoletto* and—after two forty-five-minute halves—ended with his signature aria, "Nessun Dorma" from *Turandot*.

What the opera audience didn't know was that the famous tenor flirted with not coming to Indianapolis at all, despite a signed contract.

His manager called in November, concerned that the maestro might catch cold in the Indianapolis winter. "After all," the manager said, "Mr. Pavarotti would perform in the concert hall and then have to go outside to the dinner being held at the Marott Hotel to sign autographs." (We had arranged a special dinner with Pears Pavarotti for dessert.) "Then he would have to go outside again to reach the Embassy Suites to sleep. If he gets a sore throat, we could lose millions of dollars."

Author and Luciano Pavarotti signing autographs, 1986.

"What do you want us to do?" I asked.

"Build heated, covered passageways from each venue to a waiting, warm limousine."

We did as he requested, and Luciano didn't catch a cold or get a sore throat.

PART VII

HEALTH RISKS

MY MITRAL VALVE

35

In the fall of 1999, I had a routine physical examination to increase the amount of my life insurance policy. I thought that would be a good idea prior to becoming vice president and then president of the ACC, because of all the travel involved. It turned out to be a lifesaving—and almost life-ending—decision.

I had been feeling fine, exercising an hour each morning doing aerobics and weight lifting. I figured I'd zip through the routine physical exam. The insurance doctor, an older man well into retirement, listened to my chest with an antiquated stethoscope through two layers of clothing and said, "You have a heart murmur."

"Bullshit," I said. "Give me the stethoscope." I put the head of the stethoscope on my bare chest and listened. There it was: a loud, long whooshing sound that began with the *lub* and ended with the *dub*. The diagnosis was obvious. I had developed a wide-open leaking mitral valve with no symptoms whatsoever. Untreated, mitral insufficiency of this magnitude would cause heart failure, heart rhythm problems, and eventually kill me.

How did this happen? How long had I had it?

After the shock faded and my mind began to function like a cardiologist again, I put pieces together. I had been born with an insignificant congenital heart defect called mitral valve prolapse. Very common, particularly in women, MVP barely made the list of important

219

heart flaws because it caused a problem in only a very small number of those who had it. My MVP was so classic, over the years I had let medical students listen to my chest to hear the distinctive clicking sound the abnormal valve made. But it never leaked. Not until now.

I reasoned that the elevated pressure weight lifting generated had put a strain on the valve. A normal mitral valve shrugged off that extra stress, but an abnormal valve couldn't handle the added strain. One or several of the tethering tissues that kept the valve closed when the heart contracted had ruptured. Now, when my heart ejected blood, half of it flowed backward, doubling the work of my heart.

Treatment at the time was not clear: surgical repair or drugs. I tried drugs.

Two months later, in December 1999, I was sitting in the US Airways lounge at the Reagan National Airport in Washington waiting to board my plane home when my heart started to talk to me. My definition of health is when your body *doesn't* talk to you. You don't know you have a back unless it hurts, a head without an ache, a knee that isn't sore. Now I knew I had a heart. Sitting quietly, I began to feel lots and lots of palpitations—hard and irregular heartbeats—and shortness of breath. My heart was talking, no, screaming at me to do something about it, and fast.

One of the world's experts on the surgical repair of the mitral valve was Delos (Toby) Cosgrove at the Cleveland Clinic, now the clinic's CEO. I had known Toby for many years and called him from the airport lounge. I explained the problem and said I wanted surgery. Toby agreed, and we made a date for two weeks thence.

The Cleveland Clinic is one of the premier hospitals in the world. When I took care of the Saudi patients years before, it made headlines in the Indy papers. The Cleveland Clinic handles these kinds of patients daily. After my first trip to Saudi Arabia, I was feeling guilty for what I charged the family for the five-day journey. When I related that to one of the chiefs at the clinic, he laughed and said, "Not to worry. I charge that *per day* when I travel to Riyadh for a consult."

Joan and my children flew with me to Cleveland right after

Christmas 1999. Toby was squeezing me in before he left for his winter vacation. Unlike the Saudis, though, we flew coach on US Airways.

The clinic's chief of cardiology, Steve Nissen, a longtime friend and world-renowned clinician (and president of the ACC a few years after me) was my cardiologist. He did the initial evaluation. I then met with Toby, and he explained what the surgery entailed. We had a long discussion and drew multiple diagrams about where he should put his heart incisions to avoid postoperative heart rhythm problems. He was also going to use a new approach to open my chest that left the lower third of my breastbone intact, reasoning that would ease postop pain and speed healing. I emphasized I wanted a valve repair, not replacement. I had total confidence in this skilled surgeon and his staff.

The worst part of surgery for me is when you leave the prep room surrounded by loving family, and you have that lonely ride on a stretcher to the operating room. Until anesthesia puts you to sleep, the tension mounts. Waking up can also be rough as the effects of anesthesia begin to wear off and you experience pain or discomfort from the surgery. But at least you know you have survived, you are alive!

The clinic staff was superb, completely focused on patient welfare and comfort. There was lots of hands-on and touchy-feely care, so important for the patient and so reassuring, even for a cardiologist. (I wrote about that in my first novel, *The Black Widows*, to stress its importance.)

The surgery went well. Toby performed a fabulous repair (no leak almost twenty years later), and after a short stay in the recovery room, they whisked me back to my private room late that night.

That was when I could have died.

The surgical approach Toby used to expose the mitral valve cut an artery feeding the heart's natural pacemaker, the sinus node. This was an expected occurrence—not a big deal, since the blood flow to the sinus node had other sources and would repair itself—but could cause my heartbeat to fall to the low forties postop. Anticipating that possibility, Toby had left thin wires in my heart that led out through the skin and could be connected to an external pacemaker to pace my heart at a faster rate if necessary. It turned out to be necessary, since my sinus node only beat around forty per minute.

Half-dozing, with just Joan in the room, I heard the reassuring *beep, beep* from the heart monitor as the pacemaker maintained a regular rhythm at seventy-five per minute. No big deal.

Around ten o'clock that night, a nurse came into my room. I opened my eyes and watched her hang a new plastic bag of fluid.

"What's that?" I asked.

"Magnesium," she said.

"Why?"

"Your serum magnesium level is low, and your doctor ordered you to get some intravenously," she said.

"How about milk of magnesia? I'm sure my bowels would appreciate that."

She shrugged. "Doctor's orders," she said and left, with the new bag dripping its solution into my vein.

I could imagine the reasoning behind the doctor's decision. A low potassium and magnesium can cause a heart rhythm problem that goes by a fancy French name, *torsades de pointes*. It can cause sudden death. Not a good thing. I closed my eyes and attempted to go back to sleep.

Palpitations and an irregular *beep, beep* jarred me awake.

What the hell is going on? I wondered.

I strained to see the heart monitor but couldn't.

"Joan, please wheel the monitor over here so I can see it."

"Oh shit," I said, when I saw my ECG. The pacemaker was not working properly, pacing the bottom chamber of my heart some of the time but delivering electrical stimuli continuously and haphazardly. Wayward electrical stimuli could be very dangerous, especially right after heart surgery, and transform a lifesaving technology into one *triggering* sudden death.

What had happened?

I thought a moment, my head still groggy from the anesthesia and surgery. The damn magnesium infusion! It had altered my heart's response to the pacing stimuli, making it harder for each electrical impulse to pace my heart. So some of the electrical pulses failed, while others successfully stimulated my heartbeat.

"Joan, hand me the pacemaker." I was going to increase the voltage output. If my analysis was correct, my rhythm would become regular again.

Suddenly the nurse, alerted at the nurses' station by the irregular rhythm, charged into the room. She saw what I was about to do.

"No, you can't do that," she shouted. "You can't touch that pacemaker."

"What do you propose to do?"

"I've paged the doctor on call."

"I could be dead by the time he gets here."

She reached for her pager, dialed a number, and said, "Come stat. Emergency."

"Joan, hand me the pacemaker."

"No, you can't," the nurse said.

Another naysayer. "Watch me," I said.

The nurse stood helplessly as I took the pacemaker and turned up the voltage.

Beep, beep, regular as a metronome. My analysis was correct. Potential sudden death averted, I fell back into my pillow and went to sleep.

The next morning, the doctor removed the temporary pacing wires when my sinus node perked up, and I was discharged a few days later.

My recovery was uneventful after that—except for one additional problem. The experimental chest incision didn't heal, and I spent six painful months as the two edges of my chest bone rubbed against each other with every movement. Sternal nonfusion, surgeons call it. The cause is not known but may be related to excessive activity after my surgery, not giving the bone a chance to heal. For six months, I couldn't exercise and barely tolerated twisting around to reach for something or look over my shoulder. I could press one side of my sternum and feel it grind against the other side.

Finally, Yousuf Mohammed, a gifted heart surgeon at my own institution, repaired my chest with lots of baling wire and maybe a little Elmer's Glue. It's rock solid now, and I don't even trigger airport security devices scanning for metal.

Two or three years later, Steve Nissen invited me back to the clinic to give grand rounds as part of a lecture series. I began my talk with, "It's always great to come to the Cleveland Clinic, but I enjoy it more being vertical than horizontal."

SAVING YOUR SPOUSE

36

Not many married couples experience the opportunity to save each other's lives. But when it happens, the sagas become indelibly embedded in family lore and the well-rehearsed topic of countless cocktail parties.

Joan's Turn

In 1988, I was the RT Hall Lecturer of the Australian and New Zealand Cardiac Society, an honor that took my wife and me to multiple cities in both countries. Part of the lecture tour included a brief stopover in Cairns, Australia, gateway to the Great Barrier Reef.

At low tide, we walked the reef surrounding Green Island, a small coral cay less than an hour's catamaran ride from Cairns. The bell clerk at our hotel had warned us about great white sharks, not likely in the inches of water we would traverse, and to wear tennis shoes to protect our tender feet bottoms. We did so, feeling the warm water ooze between our toes as we carefully detoured around the vibrant and colorful sea life. As an enthusiastic photographer, I snapped away at an endless variety of giant clams, starfish, sponges, and sea urchins, all laid bare by the receding waters.

As we walked, my wife—always on guard for wayward critters that might cross her path—suddenly reached out to me. Her arm pressed against my chest, blocking further progress.

"Stop!" she said, panic in her voice.

I looked at her in surprise, about to protest her interference with my photographic documentary. Silently, she pointed at my feet. There, trapped in a tiny pool of water where I was about to plant my next step, coiled a large sea snake—the black-and-white banded sea krait, we subsequently learned. Head weaving back and forth, forked tongue tasting the air, the krait was in a menacing attack mode. Normally shy, this krait obviously objected to being stepped on.

"Oh my God," I said. I slowly—very slowly—lowered my foot and backed away. Equally slowly, the krait uncoiled and slithered away but not before I snapped a picture of its retreat.

When we returned to Cairns, the helpful bell clerk at our hotel now schooled us about the krait. "Oh, yes, it's an extremely deadly snake," he said. "The venom kills quickly, and we have no antivenom."

Score: Joan one, Doug zero.

My Turn

A few years after my surgery, Joan—not to be outdone—had hers, complete with her own set of fireworks.

I had just returned from a four-day heart meeting to find her curled up in bed. We had spoken multiple times each day during my absence, but she never let on that she was sick.

"What's the matter?" I asked.

"I don't know," Joan said. "No appetite, and I feel sort of weak. Haven't had anything to eat or drink for a couple of days, not even water."

"Stomach hurt?"

"No, but it doesn't feel right."

Disregarding the truism not to doctor your loved ones, I examined her belly. It was soft, nontender, and bowel sounds were present—all findings against an acute, serious problem like appendicitis. However, I remembered from my general medical training about a retrocecal appendix. That meant the appendix could be sitting protected behind a loop of bowel that could wall off the inflammation or rupture and mask the usual signs of appendicitis.

I told her she should have that checked. "No, I'm fine. I'll be better in the morning," she said.

She wasn't, but still resisted going for a checkup. Fortuitously, I had been scheduled for my annual exam the following day, and I prevailed on her to take my place. Reluctantly she agreed, and we went to the hospital the following morning. Our daughter took off from work to come with us.

A superb internist examined Joan and agreed with my diagnosis. "She needs an abdominal CAT scan as soon as possible. I'll call radiology to schedule it."

He started an IV and, because Joan was now having some belly pain, gave her 25 mg of Demerol IV, a narcotic painkiller. An hour or so later, radiology called. They were ready for her; send her down.

"Let me give her another dose of Demerol. All the movement will likely flare up the pain. This will take the edge off it," he said as he infused another 25 mg.

We waited for hospital transportation that took forever to arrive. I was afraid we'd miss the opening in the radiology schedule and volunteered to push Joan to radiology in a wheelchair.

That may have saved her life.

"Sure, go ahead," the internist said.

We helped her into a wheelchair, covered her legs with a blanket, and my daughter and I rolled her to radiology.

Many hospitals relegate radiology divisions to the basement, perhaps to help insulate x-ray leakage or because of the weight of the heavy equipment. This location is remote from other divisions, such as cardiology or pulmonary, where specialists routinely treat acute medical problems.

As I wheeled Joan to the CAT scan room, she suddenly cried out,

"I can't catch my breath! I can't breathe!" She started gasping for breath and struggled as her chest heaved with each wheezing attempt to inhale.

She was turning blue from lack of oxygen, and her eyes rolled back into her head as she began to lose consciousness. My wife was dying before my eyes!

The cardiologist in me burst forth reflexively. "Cardiac arrest! Call a code blue! Get me the crash cart." The husband in me sobbed, "Oh my God, Joan. No, no!"

Radiologists are superbly trained for what they do: interpret images. They are not trained to handle acute emergencies, nor are they expected to do so. The staff stood immobile, not knowing what to do.

The cardiologist in me again shouted, "Get me a blood pressure cuff. Get me an ECG machine. She needs oxygen. Where's that damn crash cart!" I wept in between commands, tears running down my cheeks, thinking about my wife dying. I was the only one there who could save her.

People were beginning to mobilize. A nurse found a blood pressure cuff, and another wheeled over the crash cart. Someone else brought over an oxygen tank, but it was bedlam.

I knew I had to perform chest compressions—CPR—for a cardiac arrest, but I couldn't do that with Joan sitting in the wheelchair. I lifted her from the chair, carried her to an x-ray table, and laid her down on her back. I had my hands on her chest ready to start pumping when her eyelids fluttered and she took a deep breath. Slowly her color pinked, and consciousness returned. She began to breathe normally—and so did I. She was going to live!

I felt her pulse. Good pressure, regular beat, normal feel. I calmed down. Husband merged with cardiologist, and I tried to make sense of what had happened.

Joan hadn't eaten and had drunk almost no fluids for several days. Demerol had dropped her blood pressure, exaggerated by the upright position in the wheelchair. As soon as I lifted her from the wheelchair and laid her flat, her pressure returned to normal, and she recovered.

I let out a long sigh and heard crying behind me. I turned to see my daughter leaning against a wall for support, weeping as if her world had collapsed—and it very nearly had.

"Everything's okay, Deb," I shouted. "Mom's going to be fine."

Just then, one of the cardiology fellows arrived in response to the code blue. He took over the remaining care, though there wasn't much to do. A nurse drew blood for chemistries and put an oxygen probe on her finger. I scanned the ECG. Normal.

The radiologist came over and said, "She needs to be moved upstairs immediately and admitted to the hospital before anything else happens."

"You got to be kidding," I said. "She's now stable and needs a CAT scan. That's why we're here."

It took some persuasion. I told him the cardiology fellow and I would stay and make sure Joan did okay. Reassured, he relented and agreed to take the x-rays.

The CAT scan showed exactly what we had suspected. The retrocecal appendix had ruptured. Joan went to surgery half an hour later and, thanks to James Madura, a superb abdominal surgeon, she did fine. What a relief.

Score tied: one to one.

I hope it stays that way—for a long time.

PART VIII

WRITING FOR GOOD TIMES AND BAD

FROM WRITING SCIENCE TO WRITING FICTION

37

I have often been asked how and why I started writing nonmedical literature after a lifetime writing science. The how is easy to explain, the why more difficult.

I think the desire to write is embedded in the DNA of many doctors. History chronicles numerous outstanding physician writers, such as Arthur Conan Doyle, W. Somerset Maugham, Anton Chekhov, and Oliver Wendell Holmes, along with many contemporary authors like Oliver Sacks, Michael Crichton, and Robin Cook, among others. It would be a privilege to stand among these literary giants. Perhaps we share the need to be creative or to relate the many patient experiences we faced as doctors.

I have been fortunate to coedit or coauthor many cardiology textbooks. One of the most successful is *Braunwald's Heart Disease: A textbook of cardiovascular medicine.* Eugene Braunwald published the first edition of this colossal work in 1980, having personally written about half the two-thousand-page tome. He invited me to write the heart rhythm section for the second edition published in 1984. I spent eighteen months writing almost a tenth of the book and have continued that effort, adding collaborators in the later editions. For the sixth edition in 2001, Gene invited me to coedit the entire book with him, joined by a colleague, Peter Libby. We have continued that effort, adding coeditors, Robert Bonow and Douglas Mann when Gene stopped editing (though he continues to add updates to the electronic version), and, most recently, Gordon Tomaselli. Gordon will replace me after the eleventh edition to be published soon.

Eugene Braunwald, author, Peter Libby (left to right), at retreat preparing for the sixth edition of Heart Disease, 1979.

I began my first electrophysiology journal in 1989. I hired and fired several managing editors who failed to meet my high standards for the journal. Finally, I approached Joan. She turned me down flat. "Work with you 24-7? Not a chance. You can't pay me enough. Thanks but no thanks."

To capture her, I had to become creative. Knowing she was burned out as a gourmet cook, having functioned in that role for many years to the point she now hated the kitchen—except for brewing coffee and storing bread in the oven—I made her an offer she couldn't refuse.

"If you become my managing editor, you can close the kitchen."

"Forever?" she asked, doubt clouding her eyes.

"Forever," I promised. "We'll eat out every night."

And a new liaison was born. She became the managing editor of my first journal, the *Journal of Cardiovascular Electrophysiology.* We nurtured the JCE from inception to become the number-one heart rhythm journal in the world.

When I abandoned JCE to start my second journal, *Heart Rhythm,* at the request of the Heart Rhythm Society, Joan took that on as well. We competed with, and then topped, JCE as *numero uno.* The Heart Rhythm Society bestowed their President's Award on both of us for our efforts.

Joan now manages *Trends in Cardiovascular Medicine.* When Elsevier asked me to become editor of *Trends,* they said I would work with the managing editor already in place as an Elsevier employee in their home office in the Netherlands. I responded that if I couldn't sleep with the managing editor, I would not accept the editorship. They relented. Joan claims this will be her last journal, but time will tell.

I began writing fiction so many years ago I hadn't yet learned how to type. I'd read a best-selling novel by a doctor and said to myself, "I can do that." It was long before computers, at a time when I dictated all my patient records, correspondence, and notes, which my secretary transcribed.

I started dictating my first novel over a handheld Dictaphone whenever I had a spare moment: on airplane flights, car trips, or whenever a creative thought struck. I brought the mini tapes home for Joan to transcribe.

As Joan typed, she improved the story by rearranging sentences and changing wording or syntax. Over time, she became my coauthor. We had countless conversations about the novel over dinner. Joan called them discussions; I called them arguments. She liked them. I didn't.

That was when the fur began to fly.

We envisioned scenes and characters differently. She'd critique a scene I wrote: "No woman would ever say that when she's making love."

I'd disapprove in like manner: "The hero can't possibly act that way when facing a killer."

The characters became so real, as did their actions and words, that we'd debate for hours what they should say or do. We discovered a lot about each other, since we were acting out our own feelings through our storytelling roles. *I never knew you thought about it that way* was a common refrain. In fact, I once suggested this approach to the head of psychiatry at IU as therapy for troubled marriages. Ours must be rock solid, because it survived these debates.

The only way we could agree on a scene or character was to compromise, a fatal tactic that blunted the sharp edges of the story or of the protagonist and trashed the very things that made the novel interesting.

In the end, we relegated this first attempt to a drawer where 110,000 words slumber peacefully, perhaps awaiting resurrection by one of us in the future, maybe sitting alongside a blazing, toasty fire during the throes of a long, cold Indiana winter.

Early on, I realized that, despite having published hundreds of medical articles and many textbooks, writing fiction was very different. In science, we strive for clarity and design most articles with an introduction that describes what we are going to present, a methods section to elaborate how we did it, a results segment to present our findings, and a discussion that recapitulates the entire experience. The reader can't miss what we are talking about.

After taking writing courses at IU, at the Iowa Summer Writing

Festival, and other places, I learned to write fiction with an eyedropper. I dribbled a little clue here, plunked another fact there, and buried a third ten pages hence so the reader enjoyed the thrill of uncovering the twists and turns of the plot, or the true nature of the hero, and concluding, "Oh my God. That's where this is going! How exciting!"

I had to learn a new way of writing to eliminate -*ly* words. *Show action rather than tell it* is the mantra fiction writers live by. "He wrenched the phone from her tight fist" rather than "He quickly took the phone from her."

I also realized I needed blocks of uninterrupted time to write fiction. For my science writing, I could spend an hour on a manuscript, put it aside to do something else, pick it up the following day to continue writing, and so forth until completion.

Not so with a novel. I needed to be in the scene, become the character, remember whether I said her hair was blonde or brown, her eyes blue or gray. I would have to reread entire chapters to be caught up again in the story before I could continue writing. It was very time-consuming and virtually impossible to do in my younger years due to the demands of my day job.

Then I would set what I had written aside for a few days or a week and revise. Always revising. I think 90 percent of writing is revising.

I identify with this story about a writer, Oscar Wilde. When a friend asked him what he did that morning, he replied, "I spent it revising a poem."

"What did you do to the poem?" the friend asked.

"I took out a comma," Wilde replied.

"What did you do in the afternoon?"

"I put it back."

I don't write poetry, but the same can be said for writing novels.

As I wrote in the preface, every author permeates fiction with personal memoirs. The final scenes in *The Black Widows* take place in Petra,

Jordan, where I experienced many of the same events that my protagonist, Zach Dayan, endured. For *Ripples in Opperman's Pond*, I combined my interactions in two trials to write the story of identical twin brothers who have very different personalities despite having the same genes. Daniel, one of the brothers, says at the beginning of the novel, "We were identical, Dorian and I, but not at all alike."

Author, tour guide, David Rosenbaum (deceased) (left to right) at Wadi Rum, near Petra, 2004.

Author, José Jalife, Sami Viskin (seated) at Wadi Rum,
near Petra, mountain climbing, 2004.

Not Just a Game was a departure from the first two novels, as it was based on history. I found it riveting to research the 1936, 1972, and 2016 Olympic games and place a family member from a three-generation family into each one of those Olympics. My research of the 1936 games led me to conclude that Hitler did not commit suicide in April 1945 but escaped to Argentina where he built his home, Estancia Inalco, just outside Bariloche, Argentina. I traveled to Bariloche this fall (2017) to investigate clues about Hitler's life and Nazi influences and to develop the foundation for a subsequent novel.

Being an unknown author in the nonmedical book genre is very frustrating, almost like being an intern all over again. I live a dichotomous life: well known in cardiology but a "Who the hell is he?" in nonmedical circles. Even after getting two presidents to read my novels (or at least accept them as gifts), my textbooks continue to far outsell my novels, probably by fifty to one.

President Bill Clinton, author, and novel, 2013.

Israeli president Shimon Peres holding novel, Eugene Braunwald, author, 2014.

The following event highlights that dichotomy.

Receiving the ESC's Gold Medal, as I mentioned earlier, was one of the highlights of my career. An event that took place three days earlier placed that recognition into perspective.

The public librarian in Columbus, Indiana, about an hour from my home, had invited me for a book signing of my second novel, *Ripples in Opperman's Pond*. Joan and I loaded about forty copies into the car, along with a few copies of my first novel, *The Black Widows,* and drove to Columbus.

Three people showed up for the book signing: an elderly man who said the font was too small to read but that the weather report had predicted rain and he needed to find a substitute venue for his usual afternoon walk—and two elderly women who said the price was too steep but that if they decided to read it, they'd buy one copy to share.

Several days later, I flew to Amsterdam to receive the Gold Medal from the European Society of Cardiology in front of several thousand people.

It's not likely I will achieve the recognition in the fiction genre that I enjoy in cardiology, but it's fun to keep trying. Perhaps someday one of my novels—or even this memoir—will achieve the same level of acceptance as one of my textbooks. If not, I won't give up my day job.

The author at Estancia Inalco, reputed to be Hitler's home after World War II.

Printed in the United States
By Bookmasters